KU-573-006

a pocketful of

RHYME

Imagination for a new generation

2006 Poetry Competition for 7-11 year-olds

YoungWriters

Scotland Vol III
Edited by Lynsey Hawkins

 Young**Writers**

First published in Great Britain in 2006 by:
Young Writers
Remus House
Coltsfoot Drive
Peterborough
PE2 9JX
Telephone: 01733 890066
Website: www.youngwriters.co.uk

All Rights Reserved

© Copyright Contributors 2006

SB ISBN 1 84602 435 8

Foreword

Young Writers was established in 1991 and has been passionately devoted to the promotion of reading and writing in children and young adults ever since. The quest continues today. Young Writers remains as committed to the nurturing of poetic and literary talent as ever.

This year's Young Writers competition has proven as vibrant and dynamic as ever and we are delighted to present a showcase of the best poetry from across the UK and in some cases overseas. Each poem has been selected from a wealth of *A Pocketful Of Rhyme* entries before ultimately being published in this, our fourteenth primary school poetry series.

Once again, we have been supremely impressed by the overall quality of the entries we have received. The imagination, energy and creativity which has gone into each young writer's entry made choosing the poems a challenging and often difficult but ultimately hugely rewarding task - the general high standard of the work submitted ensured this opportunity to bring their poetry to a larger appreciative audience.

We sincerely hope you are pleased with this final collection and that you will enjoy *A Pocketful Of Rhyme Scotland Vol III* for many years to come.

Contents

Mhairi Wheelan (11)	19
Laurie Scott (11)	19
Martha Winter (9)	20
Sarah Wheelan (9)	21
Flora Chirnside (9)	22
Christopher Bayne (10)	23
Joanne Rennie (11)	24
Molly Scott (9)	25

Kinneil Primary School, Bo'ness

Courtney Harper (10)	26
Sarah Farmer (9)	27
Jessica Auld (10)	28
Sarah Cunningham (10)	29
Christopher Hamilton (10)	30
Crystal Henderson (10)	31
Dillon Bain (10)	32
Jade Alexander (9)	32
Lewis Findlay (9)	33
Rachael Dunn (10)	34
Scott Kilgour (9)	35
Gordon Cowen (10)	36
Rohann Gilmour (9)	37
Blair Lehardy (9)	38

Kirkmichael Primary School, Blairgowrie

Tula Mayne (11)	38
Rachel Houstoun (10)	39
Annie Winton (9)	39
Siobhan Malcolmson (10)	39
Heather Wood (11)	40
Jean Massey (10)	40
Oliver Moore (8)	40
Katie Winton (11)	41
Hannah Moore (11)	41
Neil Stewart (8)	42
Fiona Van der Veldt (10)	42
Rebecca Dick (11)	42
Robyn Graham (10)	43
Stephanie Curtis (10)	43

Holly Brown (9)   43
Julie Smith (11)   44

Knightsridge Primary School, Livingston
Josh O'Neill (11)   44
Gemma-Marie Rand (11)   45
Alexander Rowland (10)   45
Shawn Wright (11)   46
Taylor Paris (11)   46
Caitlin Dyer (11)   47
Jade Mitchell (11)   47
Rachael White (11)   48
Mhairi Muir (11)   48
Darryl Beveridge (11)   49
Jody Nyguist (11)   49
Lisa Dalzell (11)   50
Danielle Melrose (11)   50
Becky Preston (9)   51

Langbank Primary School, Langbank
Sapphire Le Sage (9)   51
Heather McFarlane (9)   52
Sara Letham (7)   52
Beth Irwin (8)   53
Errin Roy (8)   53
Gavin Hemphill (7)   54
Susannah Wallwork (8)   54
Sam Ellis (8)   54
Ross Eaglesham (7)   55
Chloe Morgan (7)   55
James Lawrence (7)   55
Blair Billings (9)   56
Kyle Rodger (7)   56
Alix Reid (7)   57
Eve Lapping (7)   57
David Small (9)   57

Largue School, Huntly
Kathryn Urquhart (8)   58
Zach Leslie (10)   58
Grant Cameron (11)   58

Beth Curtis (11)	59
Conner Morison (9)	59
Charlie Trowbridge (11)	60
James Dalley (11)	60
Ryan Stephen (11)	61
Eleanor Ralph (8)	61
David Grant (11)	62
John Urquhart (11)	62
Stuart Shearer (11)	62

Lockerbie Primary School, Lockerbie

Briagh Farish (10)	63
George Rae (9)	63
Koren Boomer (10)	64
Megan Finlay (9)	65
Luke Hammond (9)	66
Callum Johnstone (10)	66
Andrew Williamson (10)	67
Lewis Walker (10)	68
Dylan Hairstains (9)	69
Christopher Gray (10)	70

Longfargan Primary School, Dundee

Ray Lynham (9)	70
Louise MacGregor (10)	71
Sean Reilly (8)	72
Jack Hamilton (9)	72
Molly Porteous (8)	73

Lynburn Primary School, Dunfermine

Daniel Beale (9)	73
Lewis Hempseed (9)	74
Megan Lafferty (9)	74
Jessie Concannon (9)	75
Blair Springhall (9)	75
Lauren Gresty (9)	76
Ryan Wilkie (9)	76
Hazel Adams (9)	77
Lorna Glancy (9)	77
Shaun Morgan (9)	78
Dani Alxander (9)	78

Natalie Lang (9)	79
Emma Dunlop (10)	79
Lauren Thomson (9)	80
Chloe Millar (9)	80
Shannon Coll (9)	81
Kieran Rashid (9)	81
Conor Gray (9)	82
Jonathan Lawrie (9)	82

Macduff Primary School, Macduff

Cameron Birnie (10)	83
Simon West (10)	83
Calum Robertson (10)	84
Kieran Livingstone (10)	84
Laura Robertson (9)	85
Jamie Croucher (10)	85
Jack Milne (11)	86
Megan Findlater (10)	86
Liam Watt (12)	87
Aaron West (11)	87
Sophie Garden (10)	88
Kristy O'Neill (10)	88
Molly Gordon (11)	89
Billy Blanchard (10)	89
Frances Hankin (11)	90
Ashley Gillies (11)	91
Amber Lorimer (11)	92
Morgan Donald (10)	92
Lorne Learmonth (11)	93
Natalie Buchan (10)	93
Matthew Cooper (11)	94
Ryan Duguid (11)	95

Meldrum Primary School, Old Meldrum

Jasmine Cooper (10)	96
Jennifer Evans (10)	97
William Billingsley (10)	98
Ross Sangster (10)	99
Sarah Anderson (10)	99
Stephanie Cowie (10)	100
Alan Shepherd (10)	101

Jonathan Aplin (11)	102
Francesca Hill (10)	103
Katie Cumming (11)	104
William Royce (11)	105
Hannah Stewart (11)	106
Loren Christie (10)	107
Thomas Holmes (10)	107
Claire Thomson (10)	108
Amy Simpson (11)	109
Gavin Moss (10)	110

Mill of Mains Primary School, Dundee

Beth Wales (11)	110
Paris Smart (11)	111
Hannah Peters (11)	111
Ashley Scott (11)	112
Daniel Duncan (11)	112
Michael Docherty (11)	113

Milton Bank Primary School, Glasgow

Mark Ross Domi (9)	113
Melissa Williams (9)	113
Chelsea Lowe (9)	113
Callum Forrester (9)	114
Shannon Traynor (9)	114
Jodie Deakin (9)	114
Cameron Weir (9)	115
Alishia Jamil (9)	115
Kieren Monteith (9)	115
Kevin Stewart (9)	116
Shantel Buist (9)	116
Aidan Guthrie (7)	116
Jennifer Doyle (8)	117

Muirhead Community School, Troon

Rhiannon Darragh (9)	117
Ross McCutcheon (9)	117
Aimee Graham (10)	118
Shannon McLaughlin (10)	118
Stewart Perry (9)	118
Hannah Nathan (9)	119

Rebecca Fanning (9)   119
Hannah Campbell (9)   119
Victoria Campbell (10)   120
Morgan Brown (9)   120
Connor Paton (9)   120
Lauren Archibald (9)   121

New Aberdour Primary School, Fraserburgh

Stacey Carpenter (11)   121
Jemma Whyte (9)   121
Ross Greig (11)   122
Heather Martindale (11)   122
Hannah McDermott (11)   123
Leah Stephen (9)   123
Keira Kewley (10)   124
Brynle Thacker (11)   124
Francesca Hasni (11)   124
Ramsay Robertson (11)   125
Alex Perkins (9)   125
Litisha-Jade Rutter (11)   126

New Lanark Primary School, Lanark

Andrew Murray (9)   126
Zach McGinnies (7)   126
Charlie Cuthbertson (8)   127
Ashley Johnston (9)   127
Euan Harvie (8)   127
Rachael Murray (7)   128
Stephen Hill (9)   128

New Pitsligo & St Johns School, Fraserburgh

Gabrielle Simpson (7)   128
Jay Robertson (7)   129
Naomi Dennis (7)   129
Ross Cowie (7)   129
Calum Lovie (7)   130

Newtonmore Primary School, Newtonmore

Fiona Pickering (9)   130
Conor Hamilton (9)   130

Class 4/5   131
Lauren Miller (8)   131
Harry Grant (10)   132
Stuart Leslie (8)   132
Calum Johnston (9)   133
Neil Stewart (9)   133
Cameron McNiven (9)   133
Alasdair Courts (8)   133
Morgan Corrieri (9)   134
Lee-Anne Menzies (8)   134
Craig MacLeod (8)   134
Emma Mitchell (9)   134
Robyn Johnson (9)   135

Olnafirth Primary School, Voe
James Thompson (10)   135
Liam Sutherland (10)   136
Alexander Johnson (9)   136
Teri MacGregor (8)   137
Kirsty Sutherland (7)   137
Lynsey Johnson (8)   138
Laynie Graham (6)   138
Lauren Anderson (7)   139
Lois Sutherland   139

Ordiquhill Primary School, Banff
Beth Mitchell (11)   140
Bradley Robertson (11)   140
Lauren Middleton (11)   141
Rachel Hirsch (11)   141
Joseph Middleton (9)   142
John Verbiest (10)   142
Samantha Smith (9)   142
Harry Edwards (11)   143
Emma Duguid (10)   143
Gabby Munro (11)   144
Laura Smith (11)   144
Taylor Wollerton (9)   145
Kenneth Cowie (9)   145
Jessica Philip (10)   145

Our Lady of the Annunciation School, Glasgow

The Poems

Poetry In Colour

Red is . . .
Red is like a field of poppies.
Red is the colour of blood.
Red is the sun at night.
Red is like a bowl of cherries.

Green is . . .
Green is the colour of grass.
Green is like summer leaves.
Green is the colour of Celtic's badge.
Green is *go* at traffic lights.

Yellow is . . .
Yellow is bright as the sun.
Yellow is like wheat in fields.
Yellow is like leaves in autumn.
Yellow is the moon's reflection on the water.

Tommy Haddon (11)
Kenmore Primary School, Aberfeldy

Poetry In Colour

Yellow is . . .
A sandy beach a mile long.
A JCB digger, digging a hole.
Or fields of corn swaying in the breeze.
Warm custard dripping off the spoon.

Red is . . .
A tall double-decker bus.
The old rusty letter box, standing there day after day.
A watermelon and it is a very nice food.
A lovely sunset at the day's end.

Green is . . .
A football pitch on a cup day.
A hedge growing and growing
Or seaweed swaying in the sea.
A jungle wild and brilliant!

Munro Fraser (10)
Kenmore Primary School, Aberfeldy

Emotion Poem

Love is . . .
Love is a pink bunch of flowers.
It tastes like a box of chocolates.
It smells like a pink rose.
It looks like a pink heart.
It sounds like sweet tunes playing.
Love is super!

Anger is . . .
Anger is a deep dark red like fury.
It tastes like bitter cranberry juice.
It smells like steam that comes from your ears.
It looks like the teacher when a rule is broken.
It sounds like teeth grinding together.
Anger feels like no one likes you.

Joy is . . .
Love is yellow like a big sun.
It tastes like a juicy, fruity sweet.
It smells like a field of flowers.
It looks like a bright blue sky.
It sounds like the calm breeze.
Joy feels like happiness.

Sarah Blackwood (11)
Kenmore Primary School, Aberfeldy

Poems Of Emotion

Joy is . . .
Joy is orange, for the rising sun.
It tastes like a juicy pear.
It smells like a field of flowers.
It looks like people playing at the beach.
It sounds like laughter.
Joy is everything.

Fear is . . .
Fear is red like devil eyes.
It tastes like soggy semolina.
It smells like a wet spaniel.
It looks like people's shadows in a dark alleyway.
It sounds like creaking trees.
Fear is people following you at midnight.

Love is . . .
Love is pink like spring tulips.
It tastes like fluffy candyfloss.
It smells like fresh-cut grass.
It looks like shining red apples.
It sounds like a lovely melody.
Love feels like a warm fire on a winter's day.

Chloe Bennett (11)
Kenmore Primary School, Aberfeldy

Poems Of Emotion

Excitement . . .
Excitement is all different colours mixed into one.
It tastes like chocolate melting in your mouth.
It smells like sweet strawberries.
It looks like floating butterflies.
It sounds like the ocean racing back and forwards.
Excitement feels like magic.

Confusion . . .
The colour is like black and white flashing.
It tastes like stale bread.
It smells like a busy street.
It looks like a car crash and you can't move.
It sounds like a humongous noise.
Confusion is like pandemonium.

Happiness . . .
Happiness is blue like the colour of the sky.
It tastes like the lovely taste of raspberries.
It smells like plums in the summer.
It looks like people rolling on grass.
It sounds like children laughing and giggling.
Happiness is like the fluffy clouds.

Bradley Baird (11)
Kenmore Primary School, Aberfeldy

Poems Of Emotion

Love is . . .
Love looks like clear blue water.
It tastes like a fresh apple.
It smells like flowers.
It looks like the best place in the world.
It sounds like birds singing.
Love feels magic!

Hate is . . .
Hate is like a black rainy cloud.
It tastes like a rotten banana.
It smells like a cloud of smoke.
It looks like an angry tornado.
It sounds like my dad in the morning.
Hate feels like wet, slimy mud.

Joy is . . .
Joy looks like a bright summer day.
It tastes like juicy grapes.
It smells like apple crumble.
It looks like everyone jumping.
It sounds like people laughing.
Joy feels like the best day ever!

Breagha Burgess (11)
Kenmore Primary School, Aberfeldy

Poems Of Emotions

Happiness is . . .
Happiness is like a white rosebud opening.
It tastes like a juicy strawberry.
It smells like a field of daffodils.
It looks like a beautiful angel.
It sounds like lots of laughter.
Happiness is the best feeling ever.

Anger is . . .
Anger is a blazing red fire.
It tastes like a bitter lemon.
It smells like a rotten apple.
It looks like the Devil's eyes.
It sounds like angry screams.
Anger feels like being slapped.

Love is . . .
Love is a field of pink roses.
It tastes like a box of lovely chocolates.
It smells like the cool summer breeze.
It looks like a beautiful diamond ring.
It sounds like a soothing melody.
Love makes you feel all tingly inside.

Rosie Thomas (10)
Kenmore Primary School, Aberfeldy

Poems Of Emotion

Love is . . .
Love is pink like a rose.
It tastes like raspberry ice cream.
It smells like sweet perfume.
It looks like a pretty face.
It sounds like a beautiful singer.
Love feels like Valentine's Day.

Anger is . . .
Anger is red like a bullseye.
It tastes like a sour lemon.
It smells like rice pudding.
It looks like dripping blood.
It sounds like someone banging.
Anger feels like crashing cymbals.

Happiness is . . .
Happiness is yellow like the sun.
It tastes like hot curry.
It smells like a sweet daffodil.
It looks like a silver ring.
It sounds like the sea moving.
Happiness feels like having fun.

Shekira James (10)
Kenmore Primary School, Aberfeldy

Poems Of Emotion

Love is . . .
Love is red like a valentine card.
It tastes like a strawberry.
It smells like a bunch of roses.
It sounds like a love song.
Love feels like you're being pampered.

Anger is . . .
Anger is red like a bloodshot eye.
It tastes like a sour sweet.
It smells like a rotten lemon.
It looks like a mad bull.
It sounds like a panting lion.
Anger feels like you are going mad.

Happiness is . . .
Happiness is yellow like a bright sunflower.
It tastes like a bowl of cherries.
It smells like a fresh green forest.
It looks like a summer morning.
It sounds like a bird singing.
Happiness feels like being with your friends.

Jessica Stephen (10)
Kenmore Primary School, Aberfeldy

Power Cut

It was Christmas Eve when the lights went out,
I felt scared so I got my torch,
And turned it on, 'That's better,' I said.
My torch went out, *oh no!*
I heard rain banging overhead
And the striking of a match from downstairs.
The rumbling of thunder and I saw lightning strike!
It went all cold, I hid under the covers.
The night went on,
When I woke up the lights were back on.

Esther Whitford (8)
Kilry Primary School, Blairgowrie

Power Cut

The whole of the house
Was as quiet as a mouse.
We were all very cold
Candles, we had to hold.

Dad went out into the rough storm
To light the fire that will keep us warm.
In the cold kitchen, we lit a gas lamp
Then Dad came in, his jeans all damp.

I felt peaceful but worried, creepy but calm
But I was really hungry when dinner time came.
We had sandwiches instead of spag bol
But we really had no warm food at all.

The food in the freezer had defrosted
The bread in the toaster hadn't toasted.
The computer and TV had gone to sleep
But my battery alarm clock still went *beep!*

When the candles were about to go down
The lights came on, I put on a frown.
It is quite worrying, scary and cold but . . .
I really, really love it when there is a power cut!

Emma Bryce
Kilry Primary School, Blairgowrie

Power Cut

It was a dark and stormy night,
Lightning struck and gave me a really big fright,
I tried to put on the light.

It was a dark and stormy night,
I lit a candle and my room glowed,
I read a book and got really bored.

It was a dark and stormy night,
My mum opened the door and said,
'Don't worry; it's just a power cut.'

Luke Channon (9)
Kilry Primary School, Blairgowrie

Power Cut

Lightning strikes
Power cut
Glowing candles
Dark and cold

Creepy shadows
Dark and cold

Orange glow
Flickering beams
Huge flame
Flickering beams

Clock ticking
Candlelit house
Pattering rain
Candlelit house

Stormy weather
No heating
Worried children
No heating

Rumbling thunder
Matches striking
Falling trees
Matches striking

Melting wax
Cosy clothes
Burning fires
Cosy clothes

Lightning strikes
Power cut.

Catriona Ferguson (11)
Kilry Primary School, Blairgowrie

Power Cut

A dreadful storm blew up in the night.
All of it gave me a terrible fright
I twist and I turn in my warm mattress bed
Then something popped into my head
My mother had told me a scary thing
Then my alarm clock started to ring
Lightning struck
Power cut.
I went downstairs and a candle was lit
I went to sit by the fire
I saw my mum trying to use the hairdryer
My dad could not make the tea
The lights had gone off, I started to get colder
I didn't feel any bolder
I put the cover over my head
There was no warmth so I hugged my very best ted.

Pyla Bird-Leakey (7)
Kilry Primary School, Blairgowrie

Power Cut

A dreadful storm blew up in the night.
Wind blowing, trees swaying, house creaking.
Crash went a tree.
Power cut!

My mum told me it was a power cut.
She lit a candle bright,
Creepy, crackling, crashing rain.
Power cut!

Crash went another tree, quiet, creepy.
Help!
Power cut!

David Ramsay (8)
Kilry Primary School, Blairgowrie

Power Cut

A terrible storm blew up in the night.
The lights started flickering, it gave me a fright.
I lit a candle to light up my room,
I really hoped that it would be over soon.

The candle glowed bright
And there were shadows against the wall
But not mine, far too tall, it was creepy!

The wind was whistling through the trees,
It was so cold,
I felt like I was about to freeze.
Raining hard outside.
Our little stream was like a waterslide.

A few minutes later, my alarm went off.
It was the middle of the night,
I really couldn't wait until it was light,
Power cut!

Caitlin Richardson (8)
Kilry Primary School, Blairgowrie

Power Cut

It was middle of winter, freezing outside
Glad I was inside.
Suddenly *bang* the telephone blew
The lights started flickering too.

Next morning the power was still off.
No hot chocolate, no toast for breakfast.
At school, no lights or heaters,
Great, straight home!

At dinner time we ate by the light of a candle.
The candle was big,
Glowing bright and flickering.
In the morning everything was normal again.

Finn McKay (8)
Kilry Primary School, Blairgowrie

Power Cut

It all started one night,
When the moon was shining bright.

My mum lit the candle bright.
As I walked around in the candlelight,
I heard a scrape and got a fright,
I held on tight with all my might.

It all started one night,
When the moon was shining bright.

Huge flame, melting wax,
The banging of my dad's axe.
Dark, cold, no heating,
I even heard my heart beating.

It all started one night,
When the moon was shining bright.

Heather Horsman (8)
Kilry Primary School, Blairgowrie

Power Cut

A dreadful storm blew up in the night.
Lightning struck!
Power cut!
I got such a fright.

Mum went downstairs to get a torch.
Lightning struck!
Power cut!
I crept downstairs and hugged Mum tight.

Mum and I sat down and listened to sounds.
Lightning struck!
Power cut!
Rain pattering, crashing, whistling wind.

Rebecca Bryce (8)
Kilry Primary School, Blairgowrie

Power Cut

A dreadful storm blew up in the night,
I was reading by candlelight.
My mum came up with a cup of tea,
Made on the stove just for me.

We went downstairs and had a game of pairs,
My dad said to me, 'Enjoying your cup of tea?'
I was listening to the storm
My dad put the fire on and the room got warm.

I love it when there are power cuts,
The door blows open and then it shuts.
We sit by the firelight
Our candles are still glowing bright.

Ross Collier (11)
Kilry Primary School, Blairgowrie

My Cat

My cat is cuddly.
My cat has big eyes.
My cat is soft and cute.
My cat's hair is spiky, like a hedgehog.
My cat is messy.
My cat is hungry like a rhinoceros.
My cat is big and good-looking.
My cat is called Storm.

Lucy Clark (7)
Kinghorn Primary School, Kinghorn

Garden

The garden is massive
And it is mushy and quiet too.
The garden is perfect too, colourful.
The garden has lots and is nice too.

Sean Halliday (7)
Kinghorn Primary School, Kinghorn

The Panda Bear

Panda bears are very cute.
They have big black eyes.
They like to eat bamboo.
Panda bears are black and white.

Panda bears are fast.
They are big and fat.
Panda bears eat lots and lots.
They are very cuddly.

They love to drink water.
They have sharp teeth.
Panda bears are warm.
Panda bears have a fluffy coat.

Andrew Reid (9)
Kinghorn Primary School, Kinghorn

Animals

My dog likes to eat his food.
My dog likes to get walks.
My dog is cute and cuddly.
My dog likes to play.
That's my dog, AJ.

Julia McGuire (8)
Kinghorn Primary School, Kinghorn

Fruit

Fruit is juicy,
And full of fun.
It's great to eat
For everyone.

Claire Mason (8)
Kinghorn Primary School, Kinghorn

Home

My home is nice.
My home is very big.
My home is cosy.
My home is full of things to do.

I have my lunch, breakfast, dinner at home.
It has a computer, TV and a DVD player.
I have my television in my room.
My family live at home.

My home is warm, I have a bed.
I play in and outside.
Home is nice, as cool as ice.
It is not cold, it is warm.
I don't want to move,
Do you?

Adam Gillespie (8)
Kinghorn Primary School, Kinghorn

Egypt

Egypt is a really hot country.
There are lots and lots of pyramids.
The windows are small to keep the heat off.

The Egyptians write in hieroglyphics.
The Nile flows through Egypt.
The Nile flooded for six weeks.
The black land is good for growing crops.

The paper was made from papyrus.
The red land is hot and sandy.
They write with funny shapes.
The poor homes were made from mud bricks.

Lucy Aitken (8)
Kinghorn Primary School, Kinghorn

A Koala Bear

A koala bear is furry.
A koala bear has big eyes.
A koala bear loves trees.
A koala bear is lovely.

A koala bear likes to play.
A koala bear has sharp claws.
A koala bear has spiky hair.
A koala bear is sweet.

A koala bear loves to eat leaves.
A koala bear is brown and grey.
A koala bear likes the sun.
A koala bear is a friend.

Jennifer Paton (8)
Kinghorn Primary School, Kinghorn

Rabbits

A rabbit is very bouncy.
A rabbit is very furry.
A rabbit is a very good pet.
A rabbit can have bunnies.

A rabbit is a cute animal.
A rabbit is good at munching food.
A rabbit has sharp claws.
A rabbit has big eyes.

A rabbit is very fast at running.
A rabbit is an animal.
A rabbit is sometimes stripy.
A rabbit lives in a hutch.

Hannah Clunie (8)
Kinghorn Primary School, Kinghorn

Eagle Chant

Neither arms nor hooves have I
But I glide through the air
And I have . . .
Talons, talons, talons!

Neither fur nor scales have I
But I hunt with care and cunning
And I have . . .
Talons, talons, talons!

Neither swords nor guns have I
But I show my prey no mercy
And I have . . .
Talons, talons, talons!

I master every movement
For I fly with speed and grace
And I have . . .
Talons, talons, talons!

Stephanie Warne (10)
Kingsbarns Primary School, St Andrews

War To Peace

The rattle of angry machine-gun fire.
The rattle of carts down a country lane.
The whistle of an anonymous shell flying overhead.
The whistling of an old, old man sitting in the sun.
The wail of the siren before the bombs fall.
The blaring of a horn at a football match.
The crying of women at the graveyard.
The laughing of women partying in the hall.
War is like a burning building
While peace is like a tropical beach!

Callum Chirnside (11)
Kingsbarns Primary School, St Andrews

The Fox Song

Neither wings nor feathers have I,
But I'm sly and cunning
And I have
Teeth, teeth, teeth.

Neither horns nor hooves have I
But I run with speed and grace
And I have
Teeth, teeth, teeth.

Neither spears nor guns have I
But I pounce with strength and weight
And I have
Teeth, teeth, teeth.

I master every movement
For I stalk, chase and steal
And I have
Teeth, teeth, teeth.

Mhairi Wheelan (11)
Kingsbarns Primary School, St Andrews

Images Of War

War is gunfire, screaming and houses burning.
Peace is waves splashing, laughing and children playing.
War is machine guns rattling, people crying and smoky skies.
Peace is birds singing, families joking and sunny skies.
War is fire, blood and friends weeping.
Peace is life, love and friendship.
War is families vanishing without a trace.
Peace, we are thankful for it, we run, we play, we laugh.
War is just one thing that we cannot afford to have.

Laurie Scott (11)
Kingsbarns Primary School, St Andrews

Through The Classroom Door

(Based on 'Ten Little Schoolboys' by AA Milne)

Ten chatty children staring at the time,
One couldn't stand it and then there were nine.

Nine chatty children taking to their mates
One was sent out and then there were eight.

Eight chatty children wishing to go to Heaven
One wished too hard and then there were seven.

Seven chatty children making up tricks,
One teacher heard them and then there were six.

Six chatty children, barely alive,
One couldn't stand it, then there were five.

Five chatty children doing their chores,
One didn't want to, then there were four.

Four chatty children with sore knees,
One went inside, then there were three.

Three chatty children, needing the loo,
One couldn't bear it, then there were two.

Two chatty children having lots of fun,
One had to go in, then there was one.

One chatty child eating a bun,
He was finished and then there were none.

Martha Winter (9)
Kingsbarns Primary School, St Andrews

Through The Classroom Door

(Based on 'Ten Little Schoolboys' by AA Milne)

Ten cheeky children started to whine,
One was sick and then there were nine.

Nine cheeky children waiting for Kate,
One couldn't stand it and then there were eight.

Eight cheeky children waiting for Heaven,
One went too early and then there were seven.

Seven cheeky children playing lots of tricks,
One got caught and then there were six.

Six cheeky children barely alive,
One fell onto the floor and then there were five.

Five cheeky children cleaning the floor,
One didn't want to and then there were four.

Four cheeky children full of misery,
One just couldn't stand it and then there were three.

Three cheeky children being told what to do,
One went *urgh* and then there were two.

Two cheeky children wishing they were done,
One didn't finish and then there was one.

One cheeky child was given a bun,
He didn't like it and then there were none.

Sarah Wheelan (9)
Kingsbarns Primary School, St Andrews

Through The Classroom Door

(Based on 'Ten Little Schoolboys' by AA Milne)

Ten talkative children staring at the time,
One saw the clock strike twelve, then there were nine.

Nine talkative children, waiting for their fate,
One fell out too early then there were eight.

Eight talkative children waiting to be eleven,
One had their birthday, then there were seven.

Seven talkative children eating pick 'n' mix
One heard the bell ring, then there were six.

Six talkative children watching TV live
One went to the toilet, then there were five.

Five talkative children looking at the floor,
One ran out the door, then there were four.

Four talkative children staring at a bee,
One got badly stung, then there were three.

Three talkative children wondering what to do,
One went to art class, then there were two.

Two talkative children thinking of having fun,
One went out to playtime, then there was one.

One talkative child, dressed up like a bun,
Suddenly a dog came running and then there were none.

Flora Chirnside (9)
Kingsbarns Primary School, St Andrews

Through The Classroom Door
(Based on 'Ten Little Schoolboys' by AA Milne)

Ten cheeky children staring at the time
One got bored, then there were nine.

Nine cheeky children waiting to be baked,
One got scared, then there were eight.

Eight cheeky children waiting to go to Heaven,
One had a heart attack, then there were seven.

Seven cheeky children making up tricks,
A teacher went by, then there were six.

Six cheeky children barely alive,
One gave a yawn, then there were five.

Five cheeky children staring at the door,
One could not bear it, then there were four.

Four cheeky children drinking tea,
One didn't like it, then there were three.

Three cheeky children needing the loo,
One gave a cry, then there were two.

Two cheeky children not having much fun,
One ran out the door, then there was one.

One cheeky child looking at the sun,
Then he became blind, then there were none.

Christopher Bayne (10)
Kingsbarns Primary School, St Andrews

Past Her Prime

Past her prime . . .
Caged,
Alone,
The monkey swings
On her own.

Past her prime . . .
Her eyes dim
Her pretty face,
Turned sore
And grim.

Past her prime . . .
Her tail hangs low.
Swaying
Freely
She dreams
And breathes
Heavy, but slow.

Past her prime . . .
Caged alone.
She listens
For the sounds
Of long-lost friends,
On her own.

Joanne Rennie (11)
Kingsbarns Primary School, St Andrews

Recipe For A Disastrous School Trip

Ingredients
One ill child
One broken-down bus
One shouting teacher
Twenty noisy children
Ten ants in a lunchbox
Three coats left on the bus
Twenty melting ice creams
One meadow
And a couple of squishy cowpats for good measure!

What to do
Carefully place the broken-down bus into the bowl and mix in one
ill child.
Add in a pinch of shouting teacher and melt for ten minutes.
Then carefully blend in one meadow with a couple of squishy cowpats.
Gently tip in ten ants in a lunchbox.
Add a hint of twenty melting ice creams
With a small serving spoon of three coats left on the bus.
Boil for an hour on gas mark four.

Remember; always get an adult to help in the kitchen.

Molly Scott (9)
Kingsbarns Primary School, St Andrews

My Promise Of Friendship

I want to be friends with you till
Black widows come to Bo'ness,
I will be your friend till Chuckie turns human,
Until trees start talking and fish start walking,
When men have babies and ladies turn to monkeys.

If we are friends I will
Take you swimming,
Buy you sweeties; take you to see graffiti walls,
I will take you to shopping malls
And buy you all you want.

I will give you a gold ring
I will pick you up when you're down,
If you want I shall give you the Queen's crown,
So that you don't frown.

I will like you more than
Vanilla ice cream,
I will like you more then when 50 Cent makes me scream,
I will like you more than doing sums,
I shall give you all my wine gums.

Courtney Harper (10)
Kinneil Primary School, Bo'ness

My Promise Of Friendship

I want to be friends
Till majorettes are no more,
Until the sky turns yellow, plus the clouds go golden,
The pencils move themselves
And my shoes turn to rock.

If we are friends . . .
When we have a race, I'll let you win first place.
I will always like you, if you like me too.
I will always be here for you
And get you what you want me to.

I will give you sweets
And I'll give you help as well.
I will give you my trampoline
And all my hope,

I will like you more than
The sun in the sky.
My mum being nice to me
And my big, bouncy trampoline.
We will be friends forever.

Sarah Farmer (9)
Kinneil Primary School, Bo'ness

Promise Of Friendship

I want to be friends with you
Till the world finds its corners
And we have to live in space.
I'd be friends with you
Till there's nothing left in the world
And we start to fade away.

If we were friends
I would take you on a £100,000 shopping spree
And buy a box of chocolates, all for free.
I would stick up for you, when you want me to
And do anything for you.

I would give you my heart and soul
And keep you safe.
Just in case you need my faith.
I would give you my beautiful, intelligent horse
And my fast red Porsche.

I would like you more than going on holiday
And watching the TV screen.
I would like you more than winning the lottery
And even doing pottery.

Jessica Auld (10)
Kinneil Primary School, Bo'ness

My Promise Of Friendship

I want to be friends with you
Till the stars turn purple
And everyone loses their hair.
Paper starts walking
And the grass turns purple.
Animals start talking
And humans grow a tail.

If we are friends
I will tell you all of my secrets
And stick up for you
When you're getting bullied
You can play with my favourite games every day.

I will give you all of my make-up
All of my money and my secret box.
I will give you my favourite princess cake
And my fluffy, cuddly toy.

I will like you more than my fluffy hamster
And my beautiful cat.
More than good food on my plate
And my favourite sweets.

Sarah Cunningham (10)
Kinneil Primary School, Bo'ness

Promise Of Friendship

I want to be friends with you till
The Earth is in a giant windmill.
Till humans grow a tail,
Even when there isn't any mail.
Chocolate comes alive,
Till my name is Ricky Clive.

If we are friends,
I will clean your shoes,
Make big Brazil lose.
I will help you with your homework,
I'll walk you to the old Kirk.

I will give you
My house, bed, TV and fish.
I will give you whatever you wish.
I will give you my green bird.
Even my cute dog,
And my super bed,
I'll sleep on a log instead.

I will like you more than
My Xbox and couch.
I'll even like you more than my tartan pouch.
I will like you better than my little town.
Even more than the Queen's crown.
This is my promise of friendship my friend,
I'll like you to the very end.

Christopher Hamilton (10)
Kinneil Primary School, Bo'ness

Promise Of Friendship

I want to be friends with you
Till humans grow a tail,
And aliens deliver the mail.
Until there is no time
And all the seas turn to red wine.

If we are friends . . .
I will be there for you, day and night.
I'll look after you if you get a fright.
I'll hold you close, and keep you safe.
In you I'll always have faith.

I will give you . . .
The moon, the stars and the rays of the sun.
The gold trophy that I won.
I will give you the clouds in the sky
Until morning is nigh.

I will like you more than
The stars in the sky
And my lovely bow tie.
I will like you more than
The world around me
And a cup of Tetley's rich tea.

Now that I have made this promise
We can be friends together forever.

Crystal Henderson (10)
Kinneil Primary School, Bo'ness

My Promise Of Friendship

I want to be friends with you
Till the world finds its corners
And we dissolve into thin air,
Until the trees go bare and the grass is fair.

If we are friends,
I will never leave your side,
And stick up for you always.
Help you with your problems
And play your favourite games.

I will give you the one and only Aston Martin V8.
I will share my pocket money
And give you my heart
And all my friendship there can be.

I will like you more than my black and spotted hound,
My comfortable wooden bed
And a shiny goldfish in a tank.

Dillon Bain (10)
Kinneil Primary School, Bo'ness

My Promise Of Friendship

I want to be friends with you till I lose my hair or die.
I'll give you all of my board games.
I will be friends with you for hundreds of years.

If we are friends, I will give you my ten-foot excellent trampoline
And also my best pair of smashing football boots.
I will give you all of my best things and also my comfortable
                                        wooden bed,
And if you need a heart, I will give you it as well.
I'll do anything for you that you want me to do.

I will like you more than my family and all of my friends at school,
More than clouds and the stars in the sky.

Jade Alexander (9)
Kinneil Primary School, Bo'ness

My Promise Of Friendship

I want to be friends with you till the Earth turns to fire,
Volcanoes start to erupt
And Earth turns to chocolate
And the grass turns blue.

If we are friends I will
Tell you my hobbies,
Help you three times a day
And play with you,
Till humans turn to clay
Through the day.

I will give you my shiny goldfish
And my shiny red crabs,
My blue box of kinx,
My extra blue bed,
My five-pound pocket money.

I will like you more than my water bed,
My PS2 and PS2 games,
My TV,
My computer,
My fish,
My crabs,
My room,
My memory card
And my Crazy Frog game.

Lewis Findlay (9)
Kinneil Primary School, Bo'ness

My Promise Of Friendship

I want to be friends with you
Till the sun gets too hot and we all start to fry,
All the plants grow as tall as mountains and until we die
And I'll be friends with you
Till all animals lose their tails.

If we are friends I will play
Your favourite games every day.
Tell you a short cut, to somewhere far away.
And help you with hard homework,
Like fractions, decimals and percentages.

I will give you my favourite sweets,
A large pizza, an entire two litre bottle of Coca-Cola.
Also I will give you a ticket to your favourite movie or concert
And I will give you a box full of teddies.

I will like you more than
My bouncy blue trampoline
My big, pink bunny rabbit
And my auntie Ruby's big, black and white dog called Toby.

Rachael Dunn (10)
Kinneil Primary School, Bo'ness

Promise Of Friendship

I will like you till
You don't need to pay for anything
Until animals walk
And paper starts to talk.

I will take you
To the pictures and swimming
To play football
And practise your shooting and ball skill
And even to my gran's
I will walk you to school.

I will give you my plasma screen TV
My PS2 and my furry dog
And my giant swimming pool
Even my Rockports.

I will like you more than the sun
Than my TV and my computer
Even my Rangers top,
Even my BMW.

Scott Kilgour (9)
Kinneil Primary School, Bo'ness

My Promise Of Friendship

I want to be friends with you till
There are no more schools,
Till gorillas roam free in Scotland,
Until fish live on land
And Scotland win the World Cup.

If we are friends
I will give you FIFA Street 06,
All the chocolate I can get,
I'll give you every bit of pizza,
You'll never have to have money again.

I will give you the sun and the moon as well,
My sixty thousand Mazda RX-8,
Give you every last football I can find
And all the crisps in the world.

I will like you more than
My two fluffy, hairy gerbils,
The National Theme Park
And even more than whales.

Gordon Cowen (10)
Kinneil Primary School, Bo'ness

Promise Of Friendship

I want to be friends with you
Till the moon stops shining,
Until the sky turns grey.
I will be friends with you until
Water stops flowing,
Plants stop growing,
Until the moon turns to cheese.

If we are friends I will
Play with you every day
I'll turn hay to clay.

I will give you . . .
My three cute rabbits,
My favourite pizza and pastas,
My favourite basketball.
I will give you all my hair baubles.

I will like you more than
My mum and dad,
My favourite chocolate ripple,
And even more than my favourite TV programme, Tracy Beaker.

Rohann Gilmour (9)
Kinneil Primary School, Bo'ness

My Promise Of Friendship

I want to be friends with you
Till humans grow a tail
And I stop biting my nails
When aliens deliver the mail.

If we are friends,
I will tell you all my secrets,
And let you feed
My nice and fluffy dog.

I will give you
My friendship and my soul.
My yummy fish and chips
And let you feed my goldfish.

I will like you more than chocolate
And my cool, blue bike.
So when I die
I will always say goodbye.

Blair Lehardy (9)
Kinneil Primary School, Bo'ness

Oh My, Oh Glory Me!

A fish was sitting on a dish,
And was asking God for a wish.
The wish of the fish was granted
And so a tree was planted.
It was planted in the sea
Oh my, oh glory me!

The tree it strived
And stayed alive.
Now if you look into the sea
You will see the tree,
Oh my, oh glory me!

Tula Mayne (11)
Kirkmichael Primary School, Blairgowrie

Ponies

When I ride Murray
He's always in a hurry.
But Charlie is so slow,
He may be has a sore toe.

My ponies eat grass,
And I see them through the glass.
Murray is very fast
And Rosebud is always last.

Rachel Houstoun (10)
Kirkmichael Primary School, Blairgowrie

I Used To Be A Fairy

I used to be a fairy,
Flying high above the trees.
But now I am a witch,
That counts in twos and threes.
I own a bumping broomstick,
It always mucks around.
It gave me blobs of pus
So now I take the bus.

Annie Winton (9)
Kirkmichael Primary School, Blairgowrie

My Dog Kylie

I have a dog called Kyle,
He has a sense of style.
When he wags his tail
He makes me smile, he never fails.
You can take him for a walk,
He sure knows how to talk.
He can run a mile,
He's my own dog Kyle!

Siobhan Malcolmson (10)
Kirkmichael Primary School, Blairgowrie

What Is A Haggis?

My family say a haggis is real.
Is it a he or is it a she?
Scots have it for their meal.
Could it live up a tree?
Some people say it's big.
Some people say it's small.
Does it know how to dig?
Does it exist at all?
What is a haggis?
I would really like to know!

Heather Wood (11)
Kirkmichael Primary School, Blairgowrie

My Little Pony Beano

I have a pony called Beano.
I can't stop hugging him.
I love him so much,
With his cheeky munch
And his cheeky crunch.
He likes to trot
And sometimes gets hot.
I love my pony
Up to the brim,
I just want to tell this to him.

Jean Massey (10)
Kirkmichael Primary School, Blairgowrie

About My Sisters

I have a sister, she's very kind.
But sometimes has an absent mind.
My other is very cool,
But sometimes cruel.

Oliver Moore (8)
Kirkmichael Primary School, Blairgowrie

What Is A Haggis?

What is a haggis?
Someone tell me!
I want to know!
I want to see!
My mum tells me
That it is not true.
My dad tells me
It's as small as my shoe.
My grandpa tells me
That it's very small.
My granny tells me
It's not very tall.
What is a haggis?
Please, someone tell me!
I want to know!
I want to see!

Katie Winton (11)
Kirkmichael Primary School, Blairgowrie

What Is A Haggis?

What is a haggis?
I would like to know.
Can you tie it in a bow?
Is it tall
Or is it small?
Does it walk
Or can it talk?
Can it play computer games
Or can you walk straight through flames?
What is a haggis?
I would like to know.

Hannah Moore (11)
Kirkmichael Primary School, Blairgowrie

A Poem In Scottish

Scule, scule bonny scule,
All the weans and teachers.
The weans write sums,
While the teachers drink tea.
The bell rings fer break,
The weans run tae the door.
A lassie gets stopped,
She's done something bad,
She's kicked another wee loon.

Neil Stewart (8)
Kirkmichael Primary School, Blairgowrie

What Is A Haggis?

My teacher told me the haggis was real.
My brother said it was a fruit you can peel.
My aunt thinks it's an eel.
My dad said, it's not real.
My sister said it was a seal
But I just want one for my meal!

Fiona Van der Veldt (10)
Kirkmichael Primary School, Blairgowrie

What Is A Haggis?

My mum says a haggis is real.
My dad is not quite sure.
My dog has it for a meal.
My brother says for a cold, it is a cure.
My sister thinks it tastes like mould
I think it deserves gold.

Rebecca Dick (11)
Kirkmichael Primary School, Blairgowrie

Birds

Birds, birds when you sing you're full of spring.
When it's winter you flutter away.
When you have babies you look after them.
You go out to look for food for them,
You teach them how to fly.
You play with them,
You have fun with them,
You watch them grow,
When you're old your kids look after you.

Robyn Graham (10)
Kirkmichael Primary School, Blairgowrie

My Puppy

I have a puppy called Jessie,
No, her second name ain't Nessie.
She's immaculately clean,
The cleanest dog you've ever seen!
OK, maybe not all the time,
You would normally see her full of grime.
So that's my dog Jessie,
And again, her second name ain't Nessie!

Stephanie Curtis (10)
Kirkmichael Primary School, Blairgowrie

The Wee Thing

He's a small wee thing with an awful big voice.
He squeals all day and he squeals all night.
He's a squealing wee thing and he never stops.
I always have to get jump up to get the wee thing to shut up.
But in the day he is a cute wee thing and he wags his tail all day.

Holly Brown (9)
Kirkmichael Primary School, Blairgowrie

The Auld Grey Fergie

The auld grey Fergie
Its days of work are o'er noo.
All day it sits at the farm
Daeing nae hairm.
I bet there wis a moose
That once used it as a hoose.
And many a cat wid sleep there tae noo all it can doe
Is watch the mice at play
As the modern tractors trundle by
The auld grey Fergie gives a sigh.

Julie Smith (11)
Kirkmichael Primary School, Blairgowrie

Sadness

If sadness was a colour
It would be a dark grotty blue,
As black as the night's curtains.

If sadness was a taste
It would be just like hot saltwater.

If sadness was a feeling
It would be as depressing as a water-filled cloud.

If sadness was a smell
It would smell as damp and soggy as the condensation from
                                                  your kettle.

If sadness was a sound
It would sound as suffocating as a strangled cry.

If sadness didn't exist
The world wouldn't be the world.

Josh O'Neill (11)
Knightsridge Primary School, Livingston

Happiness

If happiness was a colour
It would be bright yellow,
As soft as a bouncy bed.

If happiness was a taste
It would be as juicy as a strawberry.

If happiness was a feeling
It would be like a silk cushion on your face.

If happiness was a smell
It would be like a bunch of roses.

If happiness was a sound
It would be like a robin singing on Christmas morning.

Gemma-Marie Rand (11)
Knightsridge Primary School, Livingston

Relief

If relief was a colour
It would be bright, bright white
As fragile as a snowdrop.

If relief was a taste
It would be as sweet as Belgian chocolate.

If relief was a feeling
It would be as light as a feather.

If relief was a smell
It would be as fresh as poppy fields.

If relief was a sound
It would be as relaxing as a skylark's song.

Alexander Rowland (10)
Knightsridge Primary School, Livingston

What If?

What if happiness made you fly?
I would fly to the Milky Way
Or maybe Mars
Or even Planet X.

What if the universe was chocolate?
I would eat the Milky Way,
Or maybe drink the oceans
Or even eat the galaxy!

What if there was no gravity?
I would float up to the moon,
Or maybe explore space
Or even go to the sun to get a tan.

What if poems came true?

Shawn Wright (11)
Knightsridge Primary School, Livingston

My Name Is Taylor

Taylor.
It means happy, fun and outgoing.
It is the number seven.
It's like a cuddly cute pig.
It's like my little brother dancing to Gwen Stefani.
It's the memory of my mum telling me I'm lovely
And I don't need to change.
Who taught me to be myself,
She tells me I'm special and makes me feel good about myself.
My name is Taylor and I don't want to change.

Taylor Paris (11)
Knightsridge Primary School, Livingston

Sadness

If sadness was a colour
It would be drowsy blue
As dull as a foggy day.

If sadness was a taste
It would taste like bitter coffee.

If sadness was a feeling
It would be as depressing as an unfunny clown.

If sadness was a smell
It would be lonely as an empty park in winter.

If sadness was a sound
It would be as terrifying as a murder outside your window.

Caitlin Dyer (11)
Knightsridge Primary School, Livingston

Anger

If anger was a colour
It would be boiling hot red
As aggressive as the Devil.

If anger was a taste
It would taste like spicy hot peppers.

If anger was a smell
It would smell like a smoky burning fire.

If anger was a place
It would be a trap in the chamber of a volcano.

Jade Mitchell (11)
Knightsridge Primary School, Livingston

Fear

If fear was a colour
It would be deep purple
As terrifying as a murder.

If fear was a taste
It would be just like acidic vinegar.

If fear was a feeling
It would be as cold as a touch on a frosty night.

If fear was a smell
It would be like a raging fire.

If fear was a sound
It would be like an uncontrollable scream of a parent's loss.

Rachael White (11)
Knightsridge Primary School, Livingston

Fear

If fear was a colour
It would be as black as the midnight sky
As ugly as a monster from a nightmare.

If fear was a taste
It would be as sour as a lemon.

If fear was a feeling
It would be as terrifying as dark, lonely woods.

If fear was a smell
It would be as suffocating as smoke.

Mhairi Muir (11)
Knightsridge Primary School, Livingston

Joy

If joy was a colour
It would be as green as grass
As cosy as a bed.

If joy was a taste
It would be just like a sponge cake.

If joy was a feeling
It would feel as safe as Heaven.

If joy was a smell
It would be as nice as a fry up on a Sunday morning.

If joy was a sound
It would be as cheery as a football match.

Darryl Beveridge (11)
Knightsridge Primary School, Livingston

What If . . .

What if I had all the money in the world?
I would buy all the sweets in Asda.

What if I was really small?
I could have tea with my doll.

What if I was really big?
I wouldn't be able to fit in my bed.

What if all my dreams came true?

Jody Nyguist (11)
Knightsridge Primary School, Livingston

Fear

If fear was a colour
It would be dark black
As scary as a cold night sky.

If fear was a taste
It would be as sharp as a sour lemon.

If fear was a feeling
It would be as rough as sandpaper scraping across your arm.

If fear was a smell
It would be as nasty as rotten eggs.

If fear was a sound
It would be as loud as a banshee's scream.

Lisa Dalzell (11)
Knightsridge Primary School, Livingston

If Joy Was . . .

If joy was a colour
It would be tickled pink,
As rosy as cheeks can get.

If joy was a taste
It would be as juicy as a strawberry.

If joy was a feeling
It would feel as warm as hot chocolate on a cold day.

If joy was a smell
It would smell like fresh green grass.

Danielle Melrose (11)
Knightsridge Primary School, Livingston

School Zoo

The children are like monkeys
Whizzing around and hanging upside down.
The dentist is chuckling like a hyena.
Helpers sprinting round like cheetahs.
Can you hear the roars
Coming from behind the doors?
Can you guess, I know you can.
Surprisingly, I nearly ran.

Becky Preston (9)
Knightsridge Primary School, Livingston

In The World Of Weird

In the world of weird
All the girls have knees made of cheese
And the boys are as big as doors.
The girls kiss blackboards,
And the boys' feet are shaped like keys.

In the world of weird
The deer play the bongo drums,
And the blue tigers wear gel in their hair.
The zebras all play pop songs on guitars
And a mouse can scare a yellow bear.

In the world of weird
You can hear the pineapples sing,
And the pears sunbathe in the rain.
While the plums wriggle their ears
And the green strawberries eat white paper rings.

Sapphire Le Sage (9)
Langbank Primary School, Langbank

World Of Weird

In the world of weird
All the girls wear aftershave
And the boys blow bubbles out of their nose.
The girls eat rubber and blubber
And the boys brush their hair with their toes.

In the world of weird
All the horses ride on people
And the cows stand on their heads.
The hippos play tennis in Venus
And the sloths don't go to their beds.

In the world of weird
All the apples are black
And the oranges are as dry as can be.
Mangoes are square and covered with hair
And they grow on fishes in the sea.

Heather McFarlane (9)
Langbank Primary School, Langbank

Colours And Feelings

When I am angry
I feel as red as roses in a summer garden.

When I am sad
I feel as blue as water from a waterfall.

When I am lonely
I feel as brown as the autumn leaves that have fallen from a tree.

When I am happy
I feel as pink as blossom on the fruit trees in spring.

Sara Letham (7)
Langbank Primary School, Langbank

All Over My House

Above my house,
Are people walking in Heaven
And my grandpa watching over me.
Beside my house,
Is my great green and purple slide.
Below my house
Are armies of ants
And red ants getting ready to fight.
Outside my house
Is a pear tree and a huge hill
Where my friends and I play.
Inside my house
Are the sounds of the two TVs,
My toys and bears,
But best of all, there is my mum and dad.

Beth Irwin (8)
Langbank Primary School, Langbank

The Four Creepy Doors

Down the dark creepy corridor
Are many coloured doors.

Behind the dark blue door
I heard ghouls and witches casting spells on a Hallowe'en night.

Behind the bright purple door
I felt soft pillow clouds.

Behind the sunny yellow door
I can see a sunny field with berries red and blue,
And the smell of lunch being cooked.

Behind the yellow and green door
Is a new day waiting.

Errin Roy (8)
Langbank Primary School, Langbank

Colours And Feelings

When I am angry
I feel as red as a rose on a summer's day.

When I am lonely
I feel as white as a snowdrop growing in my back garden.

When I am sad
I feel as blue as my school bag.

When I am happy
I feel as orange as the sun in summer.

When I am sick
I feel as white as typing paper.

Gavin Hemphill (7)
Langbank Primary School, Langbank

Happiness

Happiness looks like children laughing after telling a funny joke.
Happiness sounds like a bird singing a tune.
Happiness tastes like a hot toffee pudding.
Happiness feels like a soft hand stroking your cheek.
Happiness smells like a garden of fruit
And if happiness could speak it would say, 'Walk into joy with me.'

Susannah Wallwork (8)
Langbank Primary School, Langbank

Anger

Anger looks like children fighting over one another's toys.
Anger sounds like shouting in the playground.
Anger tastes like a bucketful of brown bread.
Anger feels like a slap on the face.
Anger lives in a black hole in space.
And when anger speaks, it says, *'I don't like you!'*

Sam Ellis (8)
Langbank Primary School, Langbank

When I Am Angry

When I am angry
I am as orange as a flame, impossible to put out.

When I am lonely
I am as black as the midnight sky.

When I am sad
I am as purple as a bramble on a summer's day.

When I am happy
I am as yellow as the sunset going down beyond the horizon.

Ross Eaglesham (7)
Langbank Primary School, Langbank

Colours And Feelings

When I am angry
I feel as red as Santa's suit.

When I am lonely
I feel as white as a piece of ice in the water.

When I am sad
I feel as blue as my brother's bedroom.

When I am happy
I feel as pink as my mum's lipstick.

Chloe Morgan (7)
Langbank Primary School, Langbank

Mayhem

Late at night in my dark, dark bedroom,
Late at night, I see a dark, dark shadow.
Late at night, my monster asks to play with me.
Late at night, we carefully sneak out.
Late at night we go to mess about
And in the morning he is gone!

James Lawrence (7)
Langbank Primary School, Langbank

Coloured Doors

Down the dusty, dark corridor
Are many coloured doors.

Behind the shining silver door
Is the future,
Robots flying hovercrafts
Whizzing everywhere.

Behind the flame-red door
Is hell-fire burning.
The Devil shouting and leaping
Goblins, ghouls and monsters dancing.

Behind the sapphire-blue door
The calm ocean has turned into a raging storm
Whirlpools, lightning and tidal waves.
Sea life is being destroyed!

Behind the multicoloured door
Game data
A world of chaos!
Mounted warriors slicing down soldiers
An archer shooting the warrior off his horse, but they fight on!

Blair Billings (9)
Langbank Primary School, Langbank

Colours Feelings

When I am angry
I feel as red as Santa's cheeks when he's riding through the sky.

When I am lonely
I feel as white as a snowman in the snow with nothing on.

When I am sad
I feel blue as a waterfall.

When I am happy
I feel as pink as tea-roses that grow in my garden.

Kyle Rodger (7)
Langbank Primary School, Langbank

What's In The Box?

Is it . . . ?
A red, spotty ladybird running?
A colourful butterfly, fluttering?
A delicate pink dragonfly, tiptoeing?
A lumpy bumpy centipede, snoring?
A scarlet tiny tiger, boxing?
A golden snail sleeping?
A squirmy tadpole jogging?
A silver beetle running?
I don't know, let's see . . .
Argh! It's a lumpy bumpy centipede snoring!

Alix Reid (7)
Langbank Primary School, Langbank

Monster In Trouble

Late at night my monster jumps on my bed.
Late at night we sneak down the stairs.
Late at night he eats my sister.
Late at night my monster sets houses on fire
And in the morning he is gone
But my sister is back!

Eve Lapping (7)
Langbank Primary School, Langbank

Confusion

It looks like a very sunny day when children are all wrapped up.
It sounds like odd singing in the background at the supermarket.
It tastes like chips with batter.
It feels like rock hard snow.
It smells like smoke with a dairy scent.
Confusion lives in your brain and when it speaks it says, *'Duh!'*

David Small (9)
Langbank Primary School, Langbank

Bluebell Forest

Down in the forest
The sun shines through the trees
I get a nice scent of bluebells while
I walk on the orange crunchy path.
The leaves are bright green with the sun shining down on us.
Pink, blue and purple bells shine all around.
The twigs go crunch under our feet.
The trees are bright brown and the sun lights the forest through
the trees.

Kathryn Urquhart (8)
Largue School, Huntly

Dolphin Hunting

Dolphin hunting is bad.
Dolphin hunting is sad.
Killing dolphins just for flubber
Is as bad and sad and killing whales for a rubber!
It is bad and sad
I think the dolphins feel the same.
They take whales' tails and dolphins mates just for food
Should we take lives for that?

Zach Leslie (10)
Largue School, Huntly

Sheep

Shearing the sheep and marketing them.
Handling sheep is quite hard.
Iron gates are good to keep sheep in the pen.
Everybody has to help to clip the sheep.
People clip sheep in the spring so they don't get too hot.

Grant Cameron (11)
Largue School, Huntly

Free And Wild

I climbed aboard my anxious horse
Big and strong and powerful.
The day was frosty, calm and quiet
There was a breeze, a small breeze which made his tail feel
                                              long and free.
He felt excited and full of energy.
I decided to let him go wild and free.
We galloped up and up a field
A stubble field it was.
We saw a hedge, I thought *oh no!*
Was he going to make it?
But of course for my elegant horse, it was no problem.
He made it with ease.
His mouth became frothy as his hooves thundered up the field.
Up came another fence, he cleared that with ease.
The spacious field became heaven for my strong and powerful horse.
But of course we had to stop.
We turned home and when we got there,
He seemed to say thank you.

Beth Curtis (11)
Largue School, Huntly

Night Rain

I was on the aeroplane from London to Vancouver
As we landed it poured with rain.
The pilot said, 'It's painful rain, get off the plane!'
We got our bags and caught a bus
We went to where I ski.
I slipped and slid and skidded on the ice slope.
I decided that that was enough.
I went down the slope at a terrific speed
It still rained and rained that night and day.

Conner Morison (9)
Largue School, Huntly

Happiness

H appiness is one of the world's greatest feelings,
A lmost anything can make us happy; dogs, cats, funfairs, those sort
of things.
P ools make me happy but school makes me unhappy.
P laying with my friends makes me happy; lots of things make
me happy.
I like being happy and everyone else likes it too. Everyone has
something that makes them happy.
N o one likes being sad but I'm sure everybody loves being happy.
E veryone has a best friend that makes them happy.
S urprises make us really happy, seeing people from our families that
live far away.
S urprise birthday parties are one of the things that make me
really happy.

Charlie Trowbridge (11)
Largue School, Huntly

A Sensational Sport

When you are skiing down a slope
It's an amazing sensation,
When everything is peaceful
And you are slicing through soft snow,
Twisting and turning,
Gliding over bumps
And watching the glistening,
Powdery snow *whoosh* past you.
But when you finally get to the end
And you realise it's over
You just want to go down it
Again and again and again.

James Dalley (11)
Largue School, Huntly

It Stole Time, What A Crime

My dad says I'm weird,
But I don't listen to a man with a beard.
I know there's something outside,
I know it can glide.
The next day I go outside,
I was fried,
It was hot,
That's what I thought.
Suddenly I saw a black spot getting bigger,
It was as big as a digger.
Then I shouted, 'It's got three eyes
And it flies!'
It was interested in clocks
So it flew in the window
And took every clock.
It stole time,
What a crime!

Ryan Stephen (11)
Largue School, Huntly

Fairground

When I went to the fair
I saw a wheel in the air.
New rides sparkled and glinted in the night
I stared with all my might,
What a sight!
I go on a ride, Mum says, 'No!'
But I don't care, I just *go!*
How people stare
Even the mayor!
I thought I was going to die
But no, I was only up high
Whee!

Eleanor Ralph (8)
Largue School, Huntly

Dark Night

Black cat jumping
Moon shining
Frog leaping
Tree trunks standing
Stars twinkling
Toadstools growing
Black cat sleeping
Little mouse peeping
'You can't catch me,' it's saying
'In here I am staying.
Look somewhere else for your treat.'

David Grant (11)
Largue School, Huntly

My Granny

M y granny was helpful when
Y ou needed it and she was always there for you

G ardens galore, she loved them all from
R ed roses to white ones too
A nd she absolutely loved raspberries
N o one left her when she was in hospital
N o one ever did leave her and at the funeral
Y ou knew she was properly rested forever.

John Urquhart (11)
Largue School, Huntly

Cats

C ats are funny and sometimes hungry
A nd playful and sometimes scratch
T hey purr and lick themselves clean
S hining black cats, fur like soft velvet are walking down the street.

Stuart Shearer (11)
Largue School, Huntly

My Holiday

I look, I can see
The people going to the shops.
A lady at the beach.
The waves in the sea.

I touch, I can feel,
Ice cream dripping down my hand.
The warm water in the pool.
The sun shining on me.

I smell, I can sniff,
The food in a café.
A person with some chips.
The chlorine in the pool.

I wish, I can dream,
That I had a fan to cool me down.
I dream of what I did that day
And I wish that my friends could come on my holiday.

Briagh Farish (10)
Lockerbie Primary School, Lockerbie

Silverstone Race Track . . .

Has . . .
Formula 1 cars,
Motorbikes,
Loads of fans,
A lot of reporters.

Is . . .
Hot and sweaty,
Noisy and loud,
Big and wide.

Can . . .
Be expensive,

But . . .
Is a good place to be.

George Rae (9)
Lockerbie Primary School, Lockerbie

At The Beach

I listen, I can hear,
The people chatting on and on.
The children playing hide-and-seek
And others in the sea.

I touch, I can feel
The soft sand all over me.
The water splashing through my toes,
The heat of the sun.

I smell, I can sniff,
The hot dogs people eat.
The suncream on my face.
The salty seawater.

I look, I can see,
People reading magazines.
The clouds moving in the sky
And adults sunbathing.

I really like the beach,
It is one of my favourite places.

Koren Boomer (10)
Lockerbie Primary School, Lockerbie

My Garden . . .

Is
Where . . .
Plants are growing,
Animals are creeping,
Grass is green,
Butterflies are resting.

Is
Where you see . . .
Bikes getting put away,
Ladybirds laying eggs,
Butterflies flying.

Has
Plants growing,
Bugs crawling around,
Bushes getting blown.

Can
Be messy and wet,
But
I like it the way it is.

Megan Finlay (9)
Lockerbie Primary School, Lockerbie

The Concert

I listen, I can hear
The singer singing,
Guitars doing solos,
Drumsticks hitting the drums.

I look, I can see
Guitars, drums,
The stage,
The band.

I think about . . .
How it must feel to perform to so many people.
How it must feel to be a part of a great band.
How it must feel to be a brilliant guitarist or drummer.

I wish . . .
I could play the instruments like them.
I wish I could sing like the singer
But most of all I wish I could be part of the band.

Luke Hammond (9)
Lockerbie Primary School, Lockerbie

At A Football Match

I listen, I can hear
The fans cheering for Man U.
Shouting, 'Scooby-Dooby Doo go Man U'
This is because Ronaldo scored a goal.

I smell defeat because Man U are winning,
Hot dogs and burgers with salt and vinegar,
And oil from the oil leak in the stadium.

I remember Man U were losing a few years ago and guess what?
It was the very same team that they played a year ago.
It is Bayern Munich and Man U are winning five-nil.

I wish that Ronaldo did not get injured,
That Bayern Munich had not scored and Man U had more goals.

Callum Johnstone (10)
Lockerbie Primary School, Lockerbie

The Pacific Ocean

(Inspired after whale watching in the Pacific Ocean)

Flowing
Strong currents
Between the islands
Divides Vancouver
From the mainland.
Separates civilisation
From the deep.

The Sound
Filled by Canada's rivers
Home to the whales
Humpback and Orca,
Hear the Grey call.
See the bald eagle
Swift and high
Circle the rim.

As the seals
Settle on the rocks
Night falls.
The Orcas appear
Moving at speed
Shifting through waves
They hunt through the reefs.

Andrew Williamson (10)
Lockerbie Primary School, Lockerbie

The Farm

Is where . . .
Cows are milked
Hay is baled
Silage is cut
Fields are ploughed.

Is where you see . . .
Tractors working
Sheep being sheared
Farmers feeding the cows.

Has . . .
Machinery
Sheep and lambs
Cows and calves
Pigs and piglets.

Can be . . .
Messy and smelly
But is a good place to be.

Lewis Walker (10)
Lockerbie Primary School, Lockerbie

The Beach . . .

Is . . .
Hot and sunny
Sandy and wavy.

Where you see . . .
Boats and waves
Umbrellas and people
Shells and pebbles
Rocks and water
Sand and sandcastles
Fish and starfish.

Has . . .
Boats and seas
Crabs and sand
And ice cream.

Can be . . .
Wet and soggy
Sunny and warm
And busy.

Dylan Hairstains (9)
Lockerbie Primary School, Lockerbie

The Traditional Scottish Bagpipes

I look, I can see
My priceless shiny bagpipes
Looking cool on my precious
Original display chair.

I touch, I can feel
The hard smooth wood
The soft fabric bag cover
And most of all the incredible feel of silver.

I think all about
The different types of tunes
The unusual things like hemp, reeds and valves
Can I be a world champion?

I listen, I can hear
I know they are valuable
But this is because they have a great zing
Although I know I can truly make them sing!

Christopher Gray (10)
Lockerbie Primary School, Lockerbie

Transport

T rains are fast
R overs are a type of car
A eroplanes fly high
N issan are a car company
S hips sail on seas
P assengers go on transport
O il powers trains
R ally cars drive on mud
T ugs are a type of boat.

Ray Lynham (9)
Longfargan Primary School, Dundee

Monsters

What kind of monster would you have?
Have a think,
Would it be green, ugly and stink?

Would it be small or big?
Would it have a hat or even a wig?

Would it be pink, orange or blue?
Could it bounce like a kangaroo?

Maybe it would have brains or none at all,
Could it play cricket or volleyball?

Would it go to school or just stay at home?
Would it have family or just be alone?

How many eyes, one, two or three?
Or maybe none, it just wouldn't see.

Would it be skinny or fat?
Would it have a pet, maybe a cat?

What would it eat,
Porridge or meat or maybe a seat?

What kind of hobbies would it have?
Stomping or squishing a baby calf?

No way, don't worry, that would be daft,
This is my monster poem
I hope it made you laugh!

Louise MacGregor (10)
Longfargan Primary School, Dundee

Dragon's Cave

Dragon's cave, dragon's cave
How very dark and cold
All alone with nothing to do and nowhere to go
But hunting at night and resting in daylight.
Dragon's cave, dragon's cave
Why do you serve the knight that slayed you?
For all eternity which made you very angry.
Dragon's cave, dragon's cave
What will you do?
There's nothing to do and nothing to eat
Now your time has come and you must go,
Farewell dragon I will see you soon.
Dragon's grave, dragon's grave
Rest in peace and harmony
Be peaceful with the Lord
Wait for me until I be with you.

Sean Reilly (8)
Longfargan Primary School, Dundee

Happiness

Happiness is being happy
Happiness is having fun
Happiness is playing with friends
Happiness is building dens.

Happiness is telling jokes
Happiness is making Coke floats
Happiness is making new friends
Happiness is sometimes funny.

Happiness is playing happily
Happiness is chatting with friends
Happiness is bathing in the sun
Happiness is mainly having fun!

Jack Hamilton (9)
Longfargan Primary School, Dundee

Dreamland

Do you ever wonder what happens in dreamland?
Ripe grapes hang on every single tree.
Elves run here and there looking for homes.
Angels float about in the air.
Most of the dream fairies live there.

Loads of leaves lie everywhere.
Adorable horses trot in and out of open tree trunks.
Nobody usually goes there.
Don't go there if you're listening.

Every night a new dream comes.
Xmas is the time of year when most dreams come to dreamlands.
Ice-cold is never it, for dreamlands are always hot.
The trees are covered in sparkling leaves,
Millions of clouds and rivers you'll find.
Every dream is a good one.
Never is there a bad dream.
Dreamlands lots of fun!

Molly Porteous (8)
Longfargan Primary School, Dundee

Home From School

Seeing my mum's handbag on the stair
Like a mountaineer on a mountain
Taller than the clouds
Seeing all the moist fruit in the mirrored, metal fruit bowl.

Hearing Pastel whimpering for her food
At 16.59, a minute early!
Hearing the TV blasting in my face.

Smelling a mouth-watering meal
Smelling chips like hot fire
Burning in front of me.

Daniel Beale (9)
Lynburn Primary School, Dunfermine

Home From School

Hearing my dog Bandit barking
Even before we walk in the door
Hearing my wee brother shouting like he's seen a ghost
Hearing Piper scratching like he wants to eat me.

Seeing my huge brother playing Pro Evolution Soccer 4
2-1 up to him
Seeing one delicious banana left
And me and my brother racing to get it
Seeing my room moving around like I went into the wrong one.

Smelling mince and tatties like Jamie Oliver's cooking
Smelling overripe bananas in the metal fruit bowl
Smelling my mum polishing the glass tables and sparkling windows.

Eating my delicious fresh banana
Eating scrumptious mince and tatties with brown bread
Eating my 20p mix-up
While I put my SPL stickers in my book.

Lewis Hempseed (9)
Lynburn Primary School, Dunfermine

Home From School

Seeing my cute tiny rabbit thumping around his hutch waiting for me
Seeing my cuddly fluffy toys sitting still, peacefully and calm
Seeing silver cars zooming about, flashing in the sunlight.

Hearing my fish tank buzzing as the bubbles pop on the surface
                                                    of the water
Hearing the computer blaring away as I leave it on
Hearing my mum shout to me,
'Hurry up and get changed or we will be late!'

Smelling clean, fresh air as I go outside
Smelling hot, runny chocolate brownies.

Megan Lafferty (9)
Lynburn Primary School, Dunfermine

Home From School

Hearing my dogs barking loudly
Like a screaming girl
Hearing my mum washing and drying the dishes
Glittering like gold.

Seeing my multicoloured bedroom
As colourful as a rainbow
Seeing the two of my dashing dogs
Waiting for me to come in the house.

Smelling sweetly my tomato soup dinner
Waiting to eat it
Smelling the amazing air freshener
In my bathroom like a beautiful rose.

Feeling my well-behaved dogs
Waiting for a sweet stroke from me
Feeling my marvellous mum
Like a warm, cuddly toy.

Jessie Concannon (9)
Lynburn Primary School, Dunfermine

Home From School

Seeing a big black cat bolting it
Like it's been hit by a stick of flaming fire
Seeing an enormous box of squidgy Haribos looking right at me.

Hearing cheering on the TV
Like a group of grey grumpy elephants
Hearing my mini mobile phone vibrating
Because my friend is calling me.

Smelling bowfin garlic when you open the freezing fridge
Smelling curry cooking
And potatoes in a chip pan bubbling away.

Blair Springhall (9)
Lynburn Primary School, Dunfermine

Home From School

Seeing sweet, fluffy, as cute as a newborn baby, cuddly toys
Seeing my educational and wicked PC
As heavy as a bag of bricks.

Hearing my dad's music blaring and rocking
Hearing car alarms going off as annoying as David
When Wales win the rugby!

Tasting delicious chocolate, yummy
Tasting sweet, fizzy pop as good as any sweet.

Smelling Chloe perfume ooh la la!
Smelling lavender room spray, sweet.

Feeling comfy furniture as soft as a leather suite
Feeling my Barbie and Polly dolls, wonderful.

Lauren Gresty (9)
Lynburn Primary School, Dunfermine

Home From School

Hearing my sister screaming at my mum nearly all day long
Hearing the radio speaking from when I get home until I go to sleep
Hearing the TV as loud as a foghorn
And then the volume goes as low as a mouse squeaking.

Seeing Lucy growling at cats going through the garden as fast as
a fighter jet
Seeing my mum chatting on the phone to my dad for an hour
Seeing my computer with MSN on the screen as good as graphics
can be.

Smelling a packet of delicious ready salted crisps
Smelling a candle as strong as a stink bomb
Smelling hot chocolate being made for me.

Ryan Wilkie (9)
Lynburn Primary School, Dunfermine

Home From School

Hearing the kettle boiling madly like a rocket
Hearing my dogs whining like starving wolves
Hearing Mum pouring perfect, steaming tea
Hearing the TV volume as loud as a rock band.

Seeing the cool TV channels flicking frantically
Seeing my sister playing great new games
Seeing Blaze waiting patiently to go for a wonderful walk
Seeing my letters lying on the bare floor
Like flowers dotted around grass-green pastures.

Smelling fresh flowers on the window sill
Like roses in a meadow
Smelling wonderful waffles
Smelling the raging oven ready to cook a delicious meal.

Tasting fresh funky fruit
Tasting ice cream as cold as the North Pole
Tasting a fantastic fish supper
Drinking a pure passion fruit drink.

Feeling a freezing metal fork
Feeling warm and appreciated on the inside
When I do things for my mum
Feeling fantastic as I lie and dream
About the next day of school.

Hazel Adams (9)
Lynburn Primary School, Dunfermine

Home From School

Tasting fizzy, lovely lemonade on my lips
Tasting the lovely sweet honey as sticky as can be

Smelling my mum's delicious dinner
Smelling my sister's perfume
Smelling the freshly cut grass

Touching my bed as I watch for my sister.

Lorna Glancy (9)
Lynburn Primary School, Dunfermine

Home From School

Seeing my little sister messing up my cupboard like a dump yard
Seeing a cute kitten in my back garden scratching away at my nets.

Hearing birds singing a song as they are flying in the blue sky
Hearing teenagers screaming down the street where I live.

Smelling fantastic pizzas in the cooker like a patch of fresh flowers
Smelling sizzling bacon in a roll in the kitchen.

Drinking fresh apple juice like Chinese apples from the market
Eating a fantastic fruit called figs.

Feeling my Xbox controller like a soft, toy teddy bear
Feeling my little sister cuddling me like an octopus.

Shaun Morgan (9)
Lynburn Primary School, Dunfermine

Home From School

Seeing my mum and dad sitting on the couch like statues in a museum
Seeing my cat Lucky lying against the burning radiator, his
whiskers twitching
Seeing Richie agree to go shopping like he was another boy.

Smelling sausage butties getting fried on the fryer
Smelling clean, fresh air like a cold wintry day
Smelling my mum's beautiful perfume as scented as a rose.

Hearing my cat miaowing for me to stroke his soft, furry tummy
Hearing the television talk and play music
Having high school boys and girls shouting to each other
Like they own the land!

Dani Alxander (9)
Lynburn Primary School, Dunfermine

The Writer Of This Poem

(Based on 'The Writer of this Poem' by Roger McGough)

The writer of this poem is
Busier than a honeybee
As strong as a huge tower
As gentle as a timid deer
As fast as a cool Ferrari
As slow as a horrid slug
As happy as a jolly lark
As silly as a cheeky monkey
As huge as a humongous giant
As cool as a funky DJ
As brainy as a crazy scientist
As friendly as a cuddly puppy
As funny as a silly rabbit
As cute as a big foot
As high as the gigantic sky
As tall as a huge ball.

Natalie Lang (9)
Lynburn Primary School, Dunfermine

Home From School

Seeing my dog lying in her big bed
Thumping her tail at me.

Hearing the TV with my dad lying on the recliner
Like a big, black dentist chair.

Smelling my cheese and tomato pizza
And prawn crackers sizzling.

Eating toasties with cheese and ham for my supper
And all the cheese melts out
Like ice cream falling off a cone.

Emma Dunlop (10)
Lynburn Primary School, Dunfermine

The Writer Of This Poem

(Based on 'The Writer of this Poem' by Roger McGough)

The writer of this poem is
As clever as a dictionary
As strong as a wrestler
As gentle as a feather
As fast as a rabbit
As slow as a tortoise
As happy as a smile
As busy as a bee
As quiet as me sleeping
As big as an elephant
As fit as a runner.

Lauren Thomson (9)
Lynburn Primary School, Dunfermine

The Writer Of This Poem

(Based on 'The Writer of this Poem' by Roger McGough)

The writer of this poem is
As big as a giant
As strong as a dinosaur
As gentle as a baby
As fast as a boy
As slow as me
As happy as my mum
As silly as my brother
As neat as me
As scary as can be
As messy as paint.

Chloe Millar (9)
Lynburn Primary School, Dunfermine

The Writer Of This Poem

(Based on 'The Writer of this Poem' by Roger McGough)

The writer of this poem is
As small as a mouse
As strong as can be
As gentle as a dog
As fast as a rocket
As slow as a wee baby
As happy as me
As silly as a sausage
As messy as can be
As neat as a bit of paper
As cool as me.

Shannon Coll (9)
Lynburn Primary School, Dunfermine

The Writer Of This Poem

(Based on 'The Writer of this Poem' by Roger McGough)

The writer of this poem is
As tall as a T-rex
As strong as King Kong
As gentle as a butterfly
As fast as a cheetah
As slow as a snail
As happy as can be
As silly as a clown
As hard as a rhino's horn
As weird as a fish
As cool as a gangster
As clever as an artist like me.

Kieran Rashid (9)
Lynburn Primary School, Dunfermine

The Writer Of This Poem

(Based on 'The Writer of this Poem' by Roger McGough)

The writer of this poem is
As tall as a flat
As strong as a T-rex
As gentle as a moth
As fast as a cheetah
As slow as a slug
As happy as can be
As silly as a dinosaur
As scary as King Kong
As cool as a gangster
As fun as a circus
A weird as a frog.

Conor Gray (9)
Lynburn Primary School, Dunfermine

The Writer Of This Poem

(Based on 'The Writer of this Poem' by Roger McGough)

The writer of this poem is
As small as a doorbell
As strong as a house
As gentle as a mouse
As fast as a fox
As slow as lava
As happy as can be
As silly as a ferret
As fast as lightning
As weak as a baby
As weird as a monkey
As funny as a clown.

Jonathan Lawrie (9)
Lynburn Primary School, Dunfermine

Rangers

I would like to play for Rangers.
I think they are the best.
The players in the team
Are the best I've ever seen.

I would have to practise every day,
And eat a lot of fruit.
I would go to bed early at night
So in the morning, I would be just right.

I would like to be the goalie
And save all the shots.
I could kick the ball really hard
More than over one thousand yards.

If I was number one
And got a good wage,
My agent would say, 'Wear a hat'
But I know I never should.

Cameron Birnie (10)
Macduff Primary School, Macduff

My Rabbit

I have a rabbit called Thumper,
He is fluffy and grey.
When he runs in the garden his feet go bump
He likes to sleep in a bed of hay.

I have a rabbit called Thumper,
He has a small fluffy tail.
He is a very fast runner
But when he sees a cat, his face goes pale.

I have a rabbit called Thumper,
I love him very much,
And when he is in the garden
He likes to sleep in his hutch.

Simon West (10)
Macduff Primary School, Macduff

James Bond

I am a future James Bond,
I like to go *bang, bang, bang!*
I like to shoot at Dr No
And cut off his head with a boomerang.

I am a future James Bond.
I like driving cars.
I like going undercover
And hanging on very high bars.

I am a future James Bond.
I like Sean Connery the best.
I like Aston Martins
And always like to dress the best.

I am a future James Bond.
At least I should be soon.
Just wait till I'm ten years older
And then I'll be over the moon.

Calum Robertson (10)
Macduff Primary School, Macduff

My Fish

When we go out and about
We always fish for salmon and trout.
My grandad and I
Don't fish in the sea
Of that there's no doubt.

Kieran Livingstone (10)
Macduff Primary School, Macduff

My Pets

My rabbit is called Buster,
I love him very much.
He spends the day inside the house,
But sleeps out in his hutch.

My hamster's name is Crackers,
He is really sweet.
He likes to run inside his ball
But mostly likes to sleep.

I have two little goldfish,
They swim inside their tank.
We put a little boat inside
But unfortunately it sank.

I've told you all about my pets,
I love them very much.
Some of them live in the house,
And one lives in a hutch.

Laura Robertson (9)
Macduff Primary School, Macduff

The Gorillaz

I think the Gorillaz are great
They live behind a black gate.
They drive a green jeep
Which isn't cheap,
But in it, they're never late.

Jamie Croucher (10)
Macduff Primary School, Macduff

Blitz!

Whoosh! Boom! Crash! Thud!
That's the sound a bomb makes, what a racket!
I must get out of my house; it's like a fiery hell.
But outside is like walking on lava.
The Junkers look like they will bomb me to China.
Red still covers the sky, I have to run away!
Yuck! There is a crater full of corpses and limbs
The smell of blood and sweat everywhere!
Oh no, Jimmy, poor mutt.
A bomb shelter, I must get in it!
I can't breathe with the smell of oil!
I yell all the way to it.
I'm in the bomb shelter, Mum is here.
The shelter may be small, but it's safe.
The all-clear siren, I survived!

Jack Milne (11)
Macduff Primary School, Macduff

Molly - My Friend

Molly has fair hair,
And bright blue eyes.
It reminds me of the stars in the skies.
When we play games, she plays fair,
And that is why I like her.

Molly is very smart,
And she loves apple tart.
She eats it along her way
And all through the day.

She is my special friend,
And I'll love her till the end.
Molly will never leave me
And that's the way it will always be.

Megan Findlater (10)
Macduff Primary School, Macduff

Blitz!

Buzzing of engines, clangs and bangs!
That's the way the bombs fall down.
There is screaming and yelling as people's houses come
clattering down.
Gravel and hot ash all over the place.
Buzz!
Here come the V1s and V2s.
People run like the wind when they see one fall from the sky,
Like an eagle chasing its prey.
Fire and smoke everywhere!
Crashes of Junkers when the AA guns shoot them down.
Ack! Ack! Ack! Ack!
Another one comes crashing down into a fiery hell.
Here I am finally at my shelter,
Safe from the planes and bombs.
People singing, dancing and enjoying themselves
To drown out the sound of the bombs until the all-clear siren sounds!

Liam Watt (12)
Macduff Primary School, Macduff

Football

A footballer I want to be,
I want to be the best.
As good as Thierry Henry
And my name is Aaron West.

I'll have to practise every day,
I get really excited
I hope in May,
I'll play
For Manchester United.

We'll win the Champions League
And every game we play,
I'll score lots of goals
And that will make my day.

Aaron West (11)
Macduff Primary School, Macduff

Space

I would like to be an astronaut,
Go all the way to space,
And when I get to the moon,
I'll see an alien face.

Twenty years later,
Guess what? I'm here!
And I see a green face
One with ginger hair.

I go up to the strange face
It has a purple nose,
When I look down to see his feet
He has blue hairy toes.

Suddenly an alarm goes off,
I wake up in my bed,
I remember a funny dream
It's still inside my head!

Sophie Garden (10)
Macduff Primary School, Macduff

My Mum

My mum is the best.
She cleans my socks and dirty frocks.
She's always the best,
And if I have to be honest, she rocks.

She's always on the go,
She hoovers all in a row.
I like the way she hugs,
As she cleans the dirty rugs.

My mum is really pretty,
She's really rather witty.
She looks after us all
When she'd rather be dancin' at the ball.

Kristy O'Neill (10)
Macduff Primary School, Macduff

My Family

Molly is my name,
Playing is my game,
I'm always the same
Happy and tame.

Dad is never mad
He's always glad,
He never makes me sad
He's not that bad.

Mum is never glum
She's the best mum.
She likes to walk and run
Not sit on her bum.

Camy is my brother
He's never any bother,
He doesn't look like my mother
I love him, he's my brother.

Molly Gordon (11)
Macduff Primary School, Macduff

My Hobby

Football is what I'm best at,
I wear the colour green,
And when I score a goal
I'm the best in the team.

And if I get thrown out of the team,
I'm sure it will just be a dream,
But if I do
I'm sure the coach will get a boo!

Football is what I'm best at
I practise day and night.
So that when I'm in the team
I'll *always* get it right.

Billy Blanchard (10)
Macduff Primary School, Macduff

Blitz!

Where is my house? Where are my friends? Where is my mum?
'Mum, Mum! Where are you?'
I must find her!
As I run I hear the air raid siren, I must get to a shelter, but I have
to find my mum.
Then I hear the noise I don't want to hear, the noise! The
ear-splitting noise!
The noise I hear every time there is an air raid!
But when there is an air raid I am normally in a safe shelter.
I look up at the sky, it looks beautiful.
It is the first thing I have seen which is pretty, the way the red runs
into the white.
But then the dark shapes swooping towards me ruin the sky.
Then I see the sky isn't so beautiful after all.
Bang, boom, crash!
The first bomb comes down, then another and another.
The smell is terrible, the gas, the tar, the burning.
Crash!
Houses are coming down all around me, I feel scared!
Look! There is a shelter, I must get in, the shelter is damp
and draughty.
The people in it don't talk at all.
Then the all-clear sounds.
I go outside and see the beautiful sky turn purple.
I see children run to their mums.
'Mum, Mum!'
Where is she? I feel alone.
'Mum! Mum! Mum! Mum!'

Frances Hankin (11)
Macduff Primary School, Macduff

Blitz!

Crash! Bang! Boom!
From one minute to the next
I was standing in a fiery hell!
There was smoke all around me,
I felt so alone and trapped!
The sky was red and yellow.
I was tired, I felt so helpless.
I rubbed my eyes to make sure I wasn't dreaming,
I looked up and saw bombers everywhere!
Then I looked down and there was blood all around my feet.
Houses were crashing down!
People screaming, people crying.
Breadbaskets falling from the sky!
I could hear crackling sounds coming, nearer and nearer!
Could it be? It must be . . .
The V1s and V2s are coming!
Before I knew it I looked up again,
The sky was darkening, it was almost jet-black.
I was hurt, I was worried, I was scared!
'Mum, Mum, where are you?'
Nothing, not a single word.
Bang!
The all-clear siren went off.
Children were running to their mums.
All I wanted was a hug.
I sat and cried then somebody sat down next to me,
'Mum! Mum!'
I finally got that hug after all,
Now I felt safe.

Ashley Gillies (11)
Macduff Primary School, Macduff

Blitz!

Crash! Boom! Bang!
My house comes tumbling down before my eyes.
There is nothing I can do.
I'm a helpless and scared child.
All alone, stuck in an air raid.
The sights are spectacular!
They're like nothing you could ever imagine.
Boom!
Suddenly the sky gets lighter.
The V1s and V2s come down at a powerful speed!
People panicking, screaming and crying as the bombs blow up!
It is like Guy Fawkes all over again!
The sky is bright because of the fire.
Orange, amber and scarlet!
It is like a fiery hell.
The streets are full of chaos.
I hide behind a pile of rubble, worried and breathless.
Then . . . all of a sudden . . . the all-clear sounds.
I come out of my hiding place and take a look at the destruction.
And cry.

Amber Lorimer (11)
Macduff Primary School, Macduff

Bumblebee Boy

When Bumblebee Boy was five
He lived in a big beehive.
He fell out of the tree
And could not see
But was glad to be alive.

As he buzzed from flower to flower
He got a shock when he saw a huge tower.
He flew up the side and in through a window,
What an achievement, so he started to limbo!
A delighted bumblebee boy.

Morgan Donald (10)
Macduff Primary School, Macduff

Blitz!

The siren has gone
Oh no!
Not another air raid.
Houses falling all around.
I am not going to get to the shelter in time.
I am scared, I am lonely, I am hurt, I am sad!
There are breadbaskets falling from behind.
I better keep running.
The sky is so bright and colourful!
Yet I am so dark and bewildered inside.
I want my mum but she is nowhere to be found.
Oh no, not a V2!
I don't think I will survive.
I can smell oil, ash and the dead.
I want to curl up and hide.
How am I ever going to find my family among the rubble?
I see someone, but is he German or is he English?
At last I am saved, it's the warden!

Lorne Learmonth (11)
Macduff Primary School, Macduff

My Brother

Greg is my brother's name,
His hair is blond in every way,
He's got blue eyes and is not very tall
But I wouldn't say he's awfully small.

I love him a lot and I always will
And I would never sell him
For a great big bill.
He plays with me
And hugs me really, really tight.
And every night
Before he goes to his bed
I give him a kiss goodnight.

Natalie Buchan (10)
Macduff Primary School, Macduff

Safe . . . At Last!

Bang! Crash! Boom!
As the German aeroplane went crashing into the sand
With a screeching sound that could blow your ears off!
There were gunshots going off everywhere,
Then I noticed that my group of fifty became a group of forty-eight!
I was nervous, would I be next?
I wasn't lonely though, my friend Gary was with me,
He was the only thing that kept me going.
He was a rock among stones.
Never scared was he, unlike me!
Then a German aeroplane came buzzing and squealing,
Dropping bombs wherever they could.
There was fire everywhere, Dunkirk was ablaze!
My group leader told us to start wading to the small boats,
Everyone took off their boots and jackets, the place was terribly whiffy!
I went into the water, it was getting deeper and deeper, I would
soon be swimming!
It was freezing!
I climbed into my small boat and ducked.
The Germans were bombing the small boats,
Many of them were capsized and this made me anxious.
We paddled along to our big cruise ship.
The war would soon be done; this experience was certainly not fun.
I got in the cruise ship, the place was mobbed.
We set off on our journey back home, having one last look at Dunkirk.
It looked just like a fireball had just exploded!
I could still smell the rotten, fleshy smell.
It was a sight for sore eyes to see.
The journey back to England seemed short, everybody was
so crushed.
This was the first time I'd slept in days.
This couple of weeks of my life have been just horrific,
But I'm glad that I am safe at last.

Matthew Cooper (11)
Macduff Primary School, Macduff

Blitz

Ack ack ack ack ack ack!
The sound of the AA guns shooting into the sky.
I am in a badly hit shelter, smoke is pouring in!
I am asphyxiated!
I exit the shelter to see the sky, it is a fiery hell!
I make a mistake,
I step out into the street.
The AA gun shells bouncing at my feet.
A V1 heading in my direction.
What to do?
I run away as fast as a coyote.
I feel as small as a mouse getting chased by a cat!
I find a not so damaged shelter.
The V1 hunting me is like a bird to its prey.
I stop!
St Paul's Cathedral.
I'm staring at the V1; it is going to destroy St Paul's Cathedral!
All men controlling defence guns are dead,
I need a new shelter, one far from the cathedral.
I find a shelter, not one bump in it.
The thing is, it is empty.
My mum will be worried sick,
She will think I'm dead!
The long, roaring sound is the all-clear siren, I am safe!

Ryan Duguid (11)
Macduff Primary School, Macduff

A Dragon In Me

I have a dragon in me
Snorting angrily,
Puffing huffily,
Menacingly breathing fire,
Snapping viciously,
Glaring annoyed,
Everyone cowers away from her,
But she doesn't care.

I have a lemur in me,
Scampering up trees,
Scurrying on the forest floor,
Nibbling on fruit,
Staring wide-eyed,
Waving her stripy tail,
People looking at her
She hides, scared.

I have a deer in me,
Lying calmly,
Waiting quietly,
Wandering peacefully,
Sleeping gracefully,
Relaxing,
Careful not to be seen.

Jasmine Cooper (10)
Meldrum Primary School, Old Meldrum

I Have An Animal In Me

I have a swan in me
Gracefully swimming
Peacefully sleeping,
Hiding quietly,
Shyly swimming past,
People calmly watch her,
Everyone sees her,
And she loves it.

I have a robin in me
Hungrily waiting,
Noisily singing,
Watching patiently,
Eating quickly,
People see her,
Noticing her red breast,
Flying away.

I have a cat in me,
Jumping and happy,
Never sleepy,
Noisily watching,
Bouncing past people,
Everyone strokes her,
Everyone knows her,
And she really likes it.

Jennifer Evans (10)
Meldrum Primary School, Old Meldrum

Rugby

Tearing through people,
Splashing through mud,
Getting tackled by big and small,
Landing with a thud.

Getting twisted and turned,
Thrown about,
Landing hard on your neck,
With a loud shout.

You've got the ball
There's a gap up ahead,
We are right beside you,
But don't get tackled, or you'll end up dead.

Now, dive on the ground,
Score a try,
After the match,
You could get a hot pie.

It's twenty-one to seven,
We are in the lead,
We'll probably win
Just hope we succeed.

We are doing well,
We are cutting through grass,
Like a lawnmower,
Now we are first class.

William Billingsley (10)
Meldrum Primary School, Old Meldrum

Animals In Me

I have a gerbil in me,
It scurries about going berserk,
Climbing with sharp claws,
Running and jumping,
Furry and little,
Drinking and eating.

I have a tiger in me,
Vicious and large,
Scaring little animals,
Sneaking around,
Growling and running,
Eating other animals.

I have a monkey in me,
Swinging from tree to tree,
Eating bananas,
Screaming and screaming,
Feeling hot and like steam,
Zooming like a lion.

Ross Sangster (10)
Meldrum Primary School, Old Meldrum

A Kitten In Me

I have a kitten in me
Jumping around in the fresh green grass
Exploring trees and places inquisitively
Playing happily in the trees
Waiting anxiously for her prey
Everyone wants to play with this jumpy, active kitten
Everyone wants to know this cool kitten
People love and play with her.

Sarah Anderson (10)
Meldrum Primary School, Old Meldrum

My Feelings

I have a hamster in me,
It's moving swiftly, but ambling
Its sharp claws digging and scratching,
Poking and prodding,
It murmurs and mutters,
It itches and aggravates,
It's sniffling and nibbling,
People want to catch it.

I have a rabbit in me,
It's hopping and running,
Nibbling and gnawing,
Poking and prodding,
And grooming,
Eating its food lazily,
It's plodding over to its water bowl,
People want to know it.

I have a bear in me,
It is waiting silently for its prey,
Hiding behind a bush,
It's brown and fluffy,
But fierce and ferocious,
So don't be mistaken,
It's blending in very well,
People want to kill it.

Stephanie Cowie (10)
Meldrum Primary School, Old Meldrum

My Personal Poem

I have a wasp in me
It has a great defence
Waiting for attack
Moving in flight
Small and tough
Hating bug spray
Stinging people painfully
People are scared of him.

I have daddy-long-legs in me
It moves swiftly
Hiding sneeringly
Running rapidly
Being annoying
Getting annoyed with people.

I have a pheasant in me
He walks smugly
He likes to jump
He's so proud
His friends are brave
He's brave as well
Everyone looks at him
But he doesn't care.

Alan Shepherd (10)
Meldrum Primary School, Old Meldrum

The Haunted House

I opened the door of the haunted house,
Nothing could be heard, not the creep of a mouse.
I went into the boiler room; it was full of mice,
I saw mice on the floor,
I saw mice on the door,
Nothing could be heard but the drip of a pipe.

I shut the door and flew into another,
It was full of books labelled A-Z.
I opened a book and felt an eerie presence
A hand touched my back and I spun around,
There was nothing there
Except a moth-eaten chair,
Nothing could be heard but the swinging curtains.

I ran out of the entrance of the terrifying library
And into a door which led into the dining room.
There on the old table was piping hot food fresh from the cooker.
Beside this there were goblets full of red wine,
An organ could be heard in the rooms beyond.

Inside the bathroom cobwebs and allsorts infested the ceiling.
In the bath, bright and red, was blood, drowning the skeleton that
lay beneath!
All that could be heard was the clap of thunder,
Down in the dungeon far below out came a shout,
'Argh!'

Jonathan Aplin (11)
Meldrum Primary School, Old Meldrum

The Haunted House

At the top of the big bleak hill there's a crooked old house,
In the crooked old house there's a dank dreary hall,
In the dank dreary hall there's an old grandfather clock,
In the old grandfather clock there are rats.

Through a door in the hall there's a dusty old room,
In the dusty old room there's a holey old sofa,
In the holey old sofa there's a family of mice!
Next door to the family of mice there's an old flickering telly,
On top of the old flickering old telly there's a faded old lamp,
Inside the faded old lamp there's a shattered glass bulb.

Out of the dusty old room into the dank dreary hall
Past the dank dreary hall into a shelf-filled place
In the shelf-filled place there's the rustling of pages,
Besides the rustling of pages there's the swaying of tattered curtains,
Behind the swaying tattered curtains there's a stub of blood-red wax.

Back in the dank dreary hall there's a huge ancient mirror,
In the huge ancient mirror there's a fierce, shaggy bear!
But the fierce shaggy bear is only a fierce, shaggy, stuffed head!
Phew!
There's some slimy cracked steps leading from the dank dreary hall,
Down the slimy cracked steps there's a giant creaking door,
Inside the giant creaking door there looms a cobweb-covered
Wicked, sneering bloodstained skeleton!

Francesca Hill (10)
Meldrum Primary School, Old Meldrum

The Haunted House

My hand touched the ice-cold door handle
I opened the door to reveal a dusty, oak staircase
The door screeched as I closed it
I stationed my foot on the floorboards
They let out a long, eerie screech
I looked up to see . . .
A colossal boar's head staring at me!
The only sound apparent to me was . . .
The whistle of the wind as it crept through the window.

Ding-ding-ding
I spun around
The grandfather clock's chimes were like deafening bangs
There was an eerie atmosphere about it
The lights flickered on and off, on and off
I stepped forward and opened a door . . .
A pale, white, terrified girl looked back at me
I let out a shriek of fear
So did she!
I clenched my sweaty fists
So did she!
I extended my arm anxiously
So did she!
I touched the bewildered girl
She touched me!
She was cold and hard
The girl looked ghostly and ghastly
The only sound apparent to me was . . .
The tremendous din of the ferocious thunder outside and . . .
The girl's heavy breathing but then . . .
She turned *nasty!*

Katie Cumming (11)
Meldrum Primary School, Old Meldrum

The Haunted House

I edged along the narrow hallway,
Opened the creaking black door to the kitchen and saw . . .
A long rusty knife hanging on the wall,
A spider crawling across the fridge,
A blood-filled sink,
An old, grey table
And I heard glass smashing on a stone-cold floor.

I slithered along the narrow hallway,
Opened the creaking brown door to the library and saw . . .
A thick and dusty old book,
A one-legged red chair,
A tinted window with a long dangling curtain,
A broken and snapped book ladder
And I heard the rocking chair creaking eerily back and forth.

I crept along the thin hallway,
Opened the large red door to the cellar and saw . . .
A chipped and dirty rocking horse,
A long and grey Christmas tree,
A crooked crate of blood-red wine,
A moth-eaten old teddy bear
And I heard the grandfather clock ticking.

I timidly walked across the narrow corridor,
Opened the small black door leading to the bedroom and saw . . .
A collapsed wooden drawer,
A shattered mirror staring back at me,
A destroyed brown radio,
A stiff and small mattress
And I heard the trees slamming against the window.

But in the library, sitting in the rocking chair
Was an ancient rotting skeleton holding a thick and dusty book.

William Royce (11)
Meldrum Primary School, Old Meldrum

The Haunted House

I walked through the front door
And at the end of the hallway there was another door
As I opened it I saw a kitchen,
An old, rusty dripping tap, the constant dripping was almost a beat.
I opened the fridge and cupboards,
All that was there was out of date food and the mice having a feast.
The room was dusty with cobwebs,
With spiders waiting for unsuspecting flies.

Up the stairs, on the door to the right,
Was the bedroom, in the corner, a four-poster bed.
The covers lay untouched,
Like they'd been like that for years.
The wardrobe was ancient,
Anyone could tell.
The light started flickering on and off,
I got out of the room as fast as I could!

Next up was the library,
So big and so quiet.
Row after row of fantastic books
But the creaking of my shoes on the floorboards was not so fantastic.
Squeaks could be heard
As rats crossed the room.
On my way out I heard the pit-pat
Of rain on the roof.

Down the steps I found a cellar
It was dark and dusty, I turned on the light.
In the centre was an old wooden chest,
With faded colours and a lock on the front,
I started to get curious,
Well, wouldn't you?
I opened it slowly, it was not locked,
And inside were *bats!*
Out of there I went as fast as the wind
Never again will I go into the haunted house.

Hannah Stewart (11)
Meldrum Primary School, Old Meldrum

My Dog Max

My dog Max he is so cute
My sis and me
Put him in a Batman suit.
But then I feel bad
Because he looks sad,
So then I give him a kiss.
My mum thinks he stinks
But it's just his food
Nobody pets him once he's had his food
He goes in an awful mood,
We all just stand there looking so crude.
My dog is as gentle as a leaf
He would lick a thief,
That's why I love him
But he is so dim.
He is so lovely but so very stupid
And that's why I think I was hit by Cupid.
He is as black as night
But is a bit light.
All my family love him and so do I!

Loren Christie (10)
Meldrum Primary School, Old Meldrum

Ropeworks

The activity centre,
Jumping and walking,
Climbing and sliding,
Swinging scarily,
The giant swing that
Leaves your stomach at the top
The rope slide, you
Zoom down like a
Cheetah,
We're at the end,
I want to go again!

Thomas Holmes (10)
Meldrum Primary School, Old Meldrum

Eagle Mum

My mum is like an eagle never missing a trick
She can spot a messy bedroom from five miles away.
But when she calms down and has a rest,
There's no other person I'd rather be with.
So that's my mum, now onto my dad.

My dad is like a grizzly bear, cuddly and protective.
He can tell the best jokes.
But when you are cheeky, oh no, you'd better stay away.
When he's home from work and he's had his tea,
He always plays a game or tells me jokes.
That's my dad, now onto my dog.

My dog thinks that he's a human.
He sleeps on the sofa,
When my mum gets up he steals her seat.
He tries to eat my toast and then licks all over my face.
I wouldn't change him for the world.
So that's my dog, now onto me.

I am like a tiger
With a fiery temper and I can be vicious!
But when I'm calm and in a good mood, I'm pretty happy-go-lucky.
When someone has upset someone I care about,
Like my best friend or my dog
Then I go on the warpath, you'd better stay clear!
So that's my family.

Claire Thomson (10)
Meldrum Primary School, Old Meldrum

The Haunted House

The sound of my footsteps on the stony path are crunching,
All there is to see is an old crooked house and the moon hiding
                                                    behind the tree.
The sky is dark and the wind is howling.
I put my hand out to knock on the big knocker but the door opens
                                                    for me.

I run into the kitchen and I see a knife with blood dripping from it,
A smashed glass,
A dripping tap,
And when I open the fridge I find a mouse nibbling on cheese.
The only sound I hear is thunder rumbling outside.

In the library I see . . .
Someone staring back at me but I find out that it is only a mirror,
A book of ghosts that when you open it ghosts come out,
A stuffed animal's head,
And a dead body.
The only sound I can hear is an owl howling outside.

Then I hear someone calling my name
So I run and run and run.

Amy Simpson (11)
Meldrum Primary School, Old Meldrum

Sister

Happy and fun.
Loving and caring.
Energetic and kind.
Beautiful and nice.
Getting the washing in,
Watching TV.
She's as fun as can be.

But sometimes she's so bored,
She sits, and just reads magazines,
Instead of being adored
By *me!*
Unless she's watching a film
She doesn't like to be annoyed by my brother.

Gavin Moss (10)
Meldrum Primary School, Old Meldrum

Fun In The Sun!

I lie on the beach; the warm breeze hits my face
Two little boys have a race up and down the beach.
It's so much fun in the hot, hot sun!

I go for a paddle in the cool blue sea,
Me and my family are having so much fun in the bright yellow sun.
I go back and lie on the sand; in the distance I hear a fast beat band.

The cool tune makes me tap my feet to the dancing beat.
I go for an ice cream with strawberry sauce on top, it tastes like
a dream
All that lovely whipped cream.
I am having so much fun in the radiant sun.

I am careful not to drop it as I walk back to my spot on the warm sand.
Then suddenly I trip and my ice cream lands right on the ground.
After all, I am not having so much fun in the sun!

Beth Wales (11)
Mill of Mains Primary School, Dundee

Laughter

Laughter is when a clown makes you laugh and you can't stop.
You laugh when you're being tickled,
You laugh when someone's cheering you up,
Or if you are watching a funny movie.
Some people live a comedy life and just love to entertain.
My favourite emotion has to be laughter, because I feel great inside
when I laugh
And it cheers me up if I'm sad.
Laughter is also the opposite of sadness which is the worst emotion.
Laughter is like a sweet pineapple, all sweet and freshly picked.
Laughter is like a gunge, all squidgy and gloopy.
Laughter is pink or yellow because they are both bouncy colours.
Laughter reminds me of the circus because every time I go
I always laugh.
Laughter is like a great song played over and over again.
Laughter is the greatest emotion you can feel.

Paris Smart (11)
Mill of Mains Primary School, Dundee

Darkness

Darkness tastes like a sharp bitter lemon,
Not sweet like a nice juicy melon.
Darkness looks as black as pitch
And you might see shadows moving like a witch.
Darkness is the colour black,
You can sometimes hear the floorboards crack.
Darkness sounds like a hooting owl
And even some wolf howls.
I can hear a tap dripping like a river
And up my back creeps a cold shiver.

Hannah Peters (11)
Mill of Mains Primary School, Dundee

The Dark Graveyard

The graveyard is scary,
The graveyard is spooky,
Although it is dark,
Would you dare to have a lookie?

I ran through it one evening
I was puffing and panting.
I listened carefully and
I heard something chanting.

I saw witches and wolves
Monsters and ghouls,
They were coming towards me
I was even scared of the bulls.

I was so scared that I ran back home
I told my gran and she said,
'Calm down, you look chilled to the bone.'

I will never forget that scary night
When I got such a fright
On Hallowe'en night!

Ashley Scott (11)
Mill of Mains Primary School, Dundee

At Night-Time

When it's dark the wolves will howl
And the grey clouds will cover the sky.
When it's bedtime the toddlers will moan and want to stay up.
The bats will come out of their creepy caves and the moon will rise.
Darkness feels like a black goblin running inside of you
And it can tastes like a big black raspberry.
Darkness reminds me of my bedtime and I want to go to sleep.
If you have nightmares don't be afraid, just fight those terrors away.

Daniel Duncan (11)
Mill of Mains Primary School, Dundee

It's Fun Time

Fun is like a juicy apple.
It is like a bungee jump.
The colour is as pure as red.
It reminds me of laughter.
It sounds like the roar of a plane.
It feels like the air rushing through your face.

Michael Docherty (11)
Mill of Mains Primary School, Dundee

The Upside Down Family

One day the Upside Down family were going to the beach.
They had their upside-down stuff and twenty sandwiches each.
Dad ate up the sandwiches, and got so very fat
He sat down on his deckchair and flattened the cat!

Mark Ross Domi (9)
Milton Bank Primary School, Glasgow

My Hamster

My hamster is called Fudge,
When she is cold, she gives a little nudge.
She runs on her wheel, it drives us all crazy,
We all wake up except for my dad, because he's very lazy!

Melissa Williams (9)
Milton Bank Primary School, Glasgow

Pancakes

Puff, puff pancakes in the frying pan,
Fling them up in the air
And catch them if you can.

Chelsea Lowe (9)
Milton Bank Primary School, Glasgow

The Little Brat!

Mum is pregnant,
Mum is fat,
She's about to have that little brat.

I'll have to babysit all night long
This can't be happening
This must be wrong.

When I came home from school one day
There he was, sleeping away.
'Pick him up,' Mum said,
I picked him up there was a burp
I kind of like this little brat!
What's going on, Mum's getting fat?

Callum Forrester (9)
Milton Bank Primary School, Glasgow

Pineapples

Once there was a pineapple hanging from a tree,
It grew and grew and grew and then there were three.
One got picked,
The other got nicked,
That left one,
And that got licked!

Shannon Traynor (9)
Milton Bank Primary School, Glasgow

Anger

Anger is like a red explosion.
It sounds like the sea on a stormy night.
Anger tastes like old fish and mushy peas.
Anger looks like the sun ready to blow.
Anger makes you feel moody.

Jodie Deakin (9)
Milton Bank Primary School, Glasgow

The Monster Who Lives With Me

The monster who lives with me,
Is a big scary animal with big teeth.
Every day I come in from school,
The big scary monster is on the chair.
Every time I look at the monster's face
I freak out!
When the monster roars, it is a big twister
Because the monster is my sister!

Cameron Weir (9)
Milton Bank Primary School, Glasgow

Fear

Fear is dark black.
It sounds like a tiger roaring.
It tastes like rotten eggs.
It smells like smelly socks.
It looks like an angry crocodile.
It feels hard and scary.
It reminds me of the bus window smashing.

Alishia Jamil (9)
Milton Bank Primary School, Glasgow

My Cat

My cat is black and white, like a zebra.
He can bite like a tiger.
He is fat like an elephant.
He eats like a pig
And he is as scared as a mouse.

Kieren Monteith (9)
Milton Bank Primary School, Glasgow

My Granny Is . . .

My granny is . . .
As blind as a bat,
As weak as a cat,
As quiet as a mouse,
As big as a house,
As wrinkled as a prune,
As warm as a day in June
I hope she'll come to see me soon.

Kevin Stewart (9)
Milton Bank Primary School, Glasgow

Love

The colour of love is pink and red.
Love sounds like robins and bluebirds.
It tastes like strawberries and cherries with a little bit of ice cream.
Love smells like strong roses.
It looks like a bright rainbow with flowers falling from the sky.
Love feels gentle and soft.
It reminds you of a song called, 'Love is in the air'.

Shantel Buist (9)
Milton Bank Primary School, Glasgow

Happiness

Happiness is the colour of joy.
Happiness is the sound of laughter.
Happiness is the taste of ice cream.
Happiness is the smell of sweetness.
Happiness feels like animal fur.
Happiness reminds me of my family.

Aidan Guthrie (7)
Milton Bank Primary School, Glasgow

The Bug Under My Bed

I have a bug under my bed,
I'm very scared.
It comes out at night to haunt me.
So I feed it and it gets bigger and bigger and bigger and then
It bursts!

Jennifer Doyle (8)
Milton Bank Primary School, Glasgow

Planets

Mercury is a magical place,
Venus is the hottest planet,
Earth is an inspiring place,
Mars is the red planet and dusty,
Jupiter has a ring around it
Saturn has thundering sounds,
Uranus is an amazing place,
Neptune is my favourite place,
Pluto is the coldest planet.

Rhiannon Darragh (9)
Muirhead Community School, Troon

Saturn

Saturn is my favourite planet
It has the most rings.
It's the second biggest planet,
And it's the sixth planet in the solar system.

It has the most moons.
It has thirty-one of them,
And out of all the planets in the solar system
Saturn's my favourite planet.

Ross McCutcheon (9)
Muirhead Community School, Troon

Spooky Space

Spooky space what a place
Where planets stay and like to play.

Spooky space looks OK,
But where would I like to stay?

Spooky space where rockets go,
I wonder what they know!

Spooky space big and black
Where the planets like to relax.

Spooky space where the sun shines bright
Why can't we have lots of light?

Aimee Graham (10)
Muirhead Community School, Troon

Space Poem

The stars rushing through the galaxy.
Rockets racing through the sky.
Comets revolving, planets changing.
Sun lighting up the dark sky.
Planets orbiting the sun.
We land on the moon in a space buggy.
Bouncing up and down on a never-ending journey.

Shannon McLaughlin (10)
Muirhead Community School, Troon

Space

S aturn has big rings
P hobos looks like a baked potato
A steroids make a belt in space
C omets fly through space
E arth is blue and green, easy to be seen.

Stewart Perry (9)
Muirhead Community School, Troon

Space Life

S pace is the place where the sun goes down
P lanets revolve, around and around
A steroids *zoom* through the night sky
C reepy, how I wish I could fly!
E xtraordinary rockets, crashing with flames.

L onely stars twinkle with their games
I nspiring black holes suck light away from space
F ascinating astronauts
E xciting Earth is blue and green, now I must go because that's
all I've seen.

Hannah Nathan (9)
Muirhead Community School, Troon

Space

Space, the dark and dull place
Where all the planets live.
Rockets whooshing in the air
And crashing on the moon.

Space has gone all quiet now
Since the rocket crashed.
All I can hear is a beeping
Noise, quite far away from me.

Rebecca Fanning (9)
Muirhead Community School, Troon

Space

S pace is gloomy, space is dull
P lanets orbiting around the sun
A steroids zooming into space
C rackling of the volcanoes
E xciting rockets banging in space.

Hannah Campbell (9)
Muirhead Community School, Troon

Sparkling

S atellites surrounding the planets
P luto shining in the dark
A stronauts bounding about
R acing asteroids, zooming around
K icking those disco balls all around
L ooking around me, all I see are shining stars
I ncredible planets and colours
N ice little twinkling stars in the sky
G lorious stars, I wish I could go back!

Victoria Campbell (10)
Muirhead Community School, Troon

Morgan, Morgan

Morgan, Morgan lives in space
Oh he says, 'It's a wonderful place.'
Asteroids and astronauts
Zooming through the air.
All the planets looking bare.
The moon shines high up in the sky
The stars twinkle in my eye.

Morgan Brown (9)
Muirhead Community School, Troon

Space

S pace shuttles zooming from place to place
P lanets revolving round and round
A steronauts landing on the moon
C omets whizzing in the solar system
E very planet *zooming* in outer space.

Connor Paton (9)
Muirhead Community School, Troon

Saturn

S aturn is the best planet of them all
A steronauts bouncing all over the place
T he planet has an empty, mouldy ground
U ranus is the closest planet to Saturn
R ed Mars, cool but empty
N ow we come to the end of my poem.

Lauren Archibald (9)
Muirhead Community School, Troon

Rabbit Run

R unning all the time
A way from Mr Fox
B ack to my burrow, as fast as I can
B ut now I'm back
I n my warm, safe home
T ogether with my family all over again.

Stacey Carpenter (11)
New Aberdour Primary School, Fraserburgh

Happy Bunny

R are rabbit hops
A ll day
B ouncy bunny
B ounces all different ways
I ntelligent bunny he is
T oday and of course every day.

Jemma Whyte (9)
New Aberdour Primary School, Fraserburgh

Steam

The wheels turn round and round
A glint, a gleam,
The grimy face of steam
Puffing, beating with the team.

Their faces beaming with the heat
The dust, the noise, it's hard to beat.
A cathedral of noise, the Castle Class
The engine's incredible mass.

On the footplate, a great commotion,
As the wheels are set in motion.
It really is a lovely sight
To see an engine pull with all its might.

How exciting as they shoot past
The green paint, the beautiful brass.
The shadow that they cast
As their day is passed.

Ross Greig (11)
New Aberdour Primary School, Fraserburgh

Chocolate

Giving up chocolate was the hardest thing I ever did
It took a long time for me to get rid
Of the mighty chocolate that was invading my brain
I knew that after giving up, I would never be the same.
My siblings teased me with chocolate bars and cakes
With shoddy Milky Ways and old-fashioned home bakes,
But I never gave up and no matter how hard
This project was to cope with, it got rid of my *lard!*

Heather Martindale (11)
New Aberdour Primary School, Fraserburgh

Acrostic Poem Nature

N ature is like a garden in
E very
W ay

Y ou hear the birds singing
E very day
A ll around you,
R udbecias grow from tiny seeds, to large,
S trong, beautiful flowers

R ound and round the garden you go,
E verything
S mells like a rose
O h you have to smell it!
L ovely scents stay in your heart
U ntil your dying day
T he feeling of the animals' fur
I s so soft and cuddly
O n summer days,
N ature is so beautiful because you can see blossom,
            the trees and bees fluttering about.

Hannah McDermott (11)
New Aberdour Primary School, Fraserburgh

Cute Fast Runners

R abbits are fast runners
A fox is just a bit faster
B ears are quite fast as well
B ut rabbits are just as cute
I think,
T hat I should be one instead.

Leah Stephen (9)
New Aberdour Primary School, Fraserburgh

Poetry Acrostic Poem

N ew games we play together.
    Fun and laughter can be heard, as we play all day.
E ngland, Wales and Scotland, we can all be together.
    Because our friendship is so strong, we will be together forever.
W e sometimes get into fights,
    But we always forgive each other and have great fun together.

Y ou can see that we are best friends,
    So come and be our friend.
E lectricity is fast but we are faster when we work together,
    Friendship is the best, you can't beat it.
A berdeen is the best football team,
    We all agree and we will watch them from our seats.
R emember, remember until we die, remember us you shall.

Keira Kewley (10)
New Aberdour Primary School, Fraserburgh

Rabbits

R abbits
A re as small as
B abies could be
B ut for so long staying
I n their burrows. When
T hey come out, they grow.

Brynle Thacker (11)
New Aberdour Primary School, Fraserburgh

Horse

H appy and hungry
O ne way of travelling
R acing at top speed
S weet and strong
E legant and graceful.

Francesca Hasni (11)
New Aberdour Primary School, Fraserburgh

New Aberdour

I am a Buchan Loon
Fas gan tae tell ye,
About a wee toon
That's afa special tae me.

There's a show every day
Doon at the bay.
Ye'll have a great time
An ye winna have tae pay a dime.

There's heeps tae dae,
There's the annual kirk walk.
An' fund raisers for the park.
Kirk services every Sunday
So come on in an pray.
An fin' its o'er,
Gan enjoy a pint, at the Dower.

We really hiv an afa giveed hall,
Far the adults meet, for a blether an' a ball.
The kids have the youth club, on a Friday night,
An some o' em get tae an afa hicht.

I am a Buchan Loon,
Fas telt ye,
About a wee toon
An' a hope ye visit soon!

Ramsay Robertson (11)
New Aberdour Primary School, Fraserburgh

Be Kind To Them

R abbits live underground, but
A re they meant to
B e found?
B e kind to them
I f they're hurt
T rust them and they will trust you!

Alex Perkins (9)
New Aberdour Primary School, Fraserburgh

Beautiful Rabbits

R abbits are cute, funny and smart, they eat
A pples, lettuce and carrots and all lovely things
B eautiful rabbits stay in a hutch or burrow
B ecause they are sweet, lovely and furry
I njections they may need
T he vet shall cure them fast as he pleads.

Litisha-Jade Rutter (11)
New Aberdour Primary School, Fraserburgh

III

I feel ill when I have a cold.
I see my eyes dimming.
I hear my mum coming up the stairs with my medicine.
I smell nothing in particular because my nose is blocked.
I touch the box of hankies.
I taste the catarrh when I cough.

Andrew Murray (9)
New Lanark Primary School, Lanark

Happiness

Happiness is a park.
I see slides, swings and a train.
I hear people laughing.
I smell doughnuts with sugar.
I touch the long ladders at the slide.
I taste the chocolate biscuits.

Zach McGinnies (7)
New Lanark Primary School, Lanark

Excited

Excitement is when I go on holiday.
I see a swimming pool.
I hear the waves crashing along the shore.
I smell the sweet seaweed.
I touch the smooth, silky sand.
I taste the salty sea air.

Excitement is when I am going out somewhere.
I see a big ice rink.
I hear children shouting and having fun.
I smell food from the café.
I touch the wet, cold ice.
I taste the lovely, warm food.

Charlie Cuthbertson (8)
New Lanark Primary School, Lanark

Frightened

Frightened is when I see a ghost.
I see shadows in my room.
I hear howling noises outside.
I smell my covers when I'm under them.
I touch my cold arms.
I taste the howling wind.

Ashley Johnston (9)
New Lanark Primary School, Lanark

When I'm Proud

Proud is when I win a medal.
I see a good life ahead and a smile on my face.
I hear people cheering for what I've done.
I smell the celebration cake that my mum's made for me.
I touch the prize that I have won.
I taste the chocolate from the cake.

Euan Harvie (8)
New Lanark Primary School, Lanark

Anger

Anger is when I want to rip everything into pieces.
I see red when I am angry.
I hear buzzing sounds in my head.
I smell a roaring fire.
I touch my toys, pick them up and throw them about in my room.
I taste blood from my lip that I have bitten.

Rachael Murray (7)
New Lanark Primary School, Lanark

Jealousy

Jealousy is when you see someone with something you want.
I see the children going to an amusement park.
I hear someone with a toy that I want.
I smell cake, sweet and yummy.
I touch someone's ball, it is soft.
I taste the sweet air of someone's candy bar!

Stephen Hill (9)
New Lanark Primary School, Lanark

Snowflake

Snowflake floating from the sky,
Don't float away
Or I will have to say goodbye.
I will build a snowman,
It will be my friend.
I will play with it
Until the end.

Gabrielle Simpson (7)
New Pitsligo & St Johns School, Fraserburgh

My Dog

My dog is Sam likes me
He gives me his paws
He likes walks
He likes playing with me
He barks at me a lot
He looks for a pat
I brush him
He loves the comb on his soft back
He follows me a lot,
My dog Sam.

Jay Robertson (7)
New Pitsligo & St Johns School, Fraserburgh

My Kitten

My little kitten
Sleeps on my bed.
When I'm at school
It snuggles up to Ted.

My little kitten
Hears me come.
He runs downstairs
And plays on my tum.

Naomi Dennis (7)
New Pitsligo & St Johns School, Fraserburgh

The Ghost

Here comes a ghost
Frightening and scaring
Flying and hiding
One day it jumped
And frightened everyone away!

Ross Cowie (7)
New Pitsligo & St Johns School, Fraserburgh

The Train

Here comes the train
Running down the tracks
Don't go on the rails
Please come back.

Sitting on the train
See all the fields
Pass all the farms
And into the town.

Here comes the train
Running down the tracks
Don't go on the rails
Please come back.

Calum Lovie (7)
New Pitsligo & St Johns School, Fraserburgh

Happiness

I feel happy . . .
When I see dogs.
I feel happy . . .
When I have friends
And when I see you
I feel *very happy.*

Fiona Pickering (9)
Newtonmore Primary School, Newtonmore

Cluck, Cluck Fat Hen

'Cluck, cluck fat hen
Have you any eggs?'
'No Sir, no Sir
Only chicken legs!'

Conor Hamilton (9)
Newtonmore Primary School, Newtonmore

Water

Life sustainer
Plant grower
Clothes washer
Flood bringer
Drought ender
Health promoter
Body cleanser
Precipitation producer
Loch builder
River filler
Home provider
Cloud burster
Storm designer
Puddle maker
Thirst quencher
Ship destroyer
Gutter runner
Devastating drowner
Cliff eroder
Canoe carrier
Rainbow creator
Wave riser.

Class 4/5
Newtonmore Primary School, Newtonmore

My Pet Hamster

H e is so cute
A nd always falls asleep on
M e
S oft and sweet I love him
T ablet is his name
E ats small, colourful pellets of hamster food
R uns and runs in his wheel.

Lauren Miller (8)
Newtonmore Primary School, Newtonmore

Alphabet Weather Poem

Angry
Black
Clouds
Darken
Every
Foggy
Gale
Hail
Is
Just
Kicking and
Light on foot
Mild
November is
Over
Punching
Quivering
Raging
Storms and
Thunder is heard
Under the covers
Very
Worried children hide while
Xylophones of thunder
Yell
Zigzag lightning fills the sky.

Harry Grant (10)
Newtonmore Primary School, Newtonmore

Happiness

When you're enjoying yourself,
Having fun times.
When you're smiling,
When you're heart is happy
When you're playing.

Stuart Leslie (8)
Newtonmore Primary School, Newtonmore

Sun

Sun shines
Scorching hot
Sparkling stream
Stunning sunset
Casting shadows.

Calum Johnston (9)
Newtonmore Primary School, Newtonmore

Snake

Snake
Long, slimy
Hisses, rattles, spits
Like an enormous worm
Reptile.

Neil Stewart (9)
Newtonmore Primary School, Newtonmore

The Tiger

'Growl, growl, fierce tiger
Have you any teeth?'
'No Sir, no Sir
I lost them eating beef.'

Cameron McNiven (9)
Newtonmore Primary School, Newtonmore

Tornado

Immeasurable, black,
Sucks, whirls, destroys
Like a massive Hoover
Whirlwind.

Alasdair Courts (8)
Newtonmore Primary School, Newtonmore

Roses Of Love

Sweet smiling valentine's roses
All the time, favourite roses.
Loving roses represent the heart, give them on special occasions to
the one you love!
People love to receive roses on special days to have as a sign of love!
On anniversaries, roses show you've remembered.

Morgan Corrieri (9)
Newtonmore Primary School, Newtonmore

The Seaside

S wimming in the cool sea
E ating chilly, cold ice cream
A t the lovely warm beach
S ee the seagulls flying in the air
I n the sea swimming with fish
D ogs not allowed
E veryone go to the seaside and have some fun.

Lee-Anne Menzies (8)
Newtonmore Primary School, Newtonmore

Little Lizard Leaps

His tongue is as long as an electric band.
His body is like a patch of green grass.
His skin makes him look as if he is a camouflaged soldier.

Craig MacLeod (8)
Newtonmore Primary School, Newtonmore

Tornado

Tornadoes are very strong winds,
They can blow your house away into the sky
If you go underground you will be safe.

Emma Mitchell (9)
Newtonmore Primary School, Newtonmore

What Was That?

Whizz! Bang! Crash!
What was that?
Zoom! Screech! Clash!
There it goes again!
Boom! Splish! Splash!
It's only the cat!

Robyn Johnson (9)
Newtonmore Primary School, Newtonmore

Snow

White like a fluffy blanket,
Clings onto the branches, like a bird.
As if the world had been painted,
Slippery,
Cold.
Animals freezing.
Birds starving to death, hunting for food,
Flakes fluttering silently, like butterflies.
Then the wind builds up . . .
And *suddenly!*
A blizzard comes,
Very thick
Like there is a big white wall in front of me
Can't see a thing outside,
Very windy.
But all of a sudden
I can just see outside
The wind is dying down
Back to the white fluffy blanket.

James Thompson (10)
Olnafirth Primary School, Voe

Snow

It's like someone is sprinkling
White powder over the ground,
It lies on the ground like a white blanket
As leafless trees stick out
Of the ground like bones reaching for the sky.
As animals huddle together
Others scrape desperately hoping to find food.
Car tracks in the snow
Look like someone has carved them.
As flakes fall to the ground
They form a soft sheet under our feet.
As the snow picks up speed
It's like a white wall blocking your way.
When the snow starts to melt I hope that
It will come again.

Liam Sutherland (10)
Olnafirth Primary School, Voe

The Raindrop

The raindrops splatter to the ground
Like God is crying.
They shine on the ground like gems,
Children splash cheerfully in the puddles.
People walk quickly as they get drenched by the cars.
Droplets cling desperately to the leaves,
The boats overflow with rain.
Happy children jumping around.
After the sun comes through and dries up all the rain.
The rain leaves glowing puddles behind.

Alexander Johnson (9)
Olnafirth Primary School, Voe

Auntie Sandra, The Extraterrestrial

'But she's got big, bulgy eyes.'
'Oh, that's just her glasses,
Nothing to worry about.'

'But she's got six thousand ears.'
'Oh, that's just her earrings,
Nothing to worry about.'

'But she's got one finger.'
'Oh, that's just a stick,
Nothing to worry about.'

'But she's got nine hundred thousand legs.'
'Oh, that's just her shadow,
Nothing to worry about.'

'But she's got a long neck.'
'Oh, that's just her scarf,
Nothing to worry about.'

Teri MacGregor (8)
Olnafirth Primary School, Voe

Auntie Ethel, The Extraterrestrial

'But she's got an eye in the middle of her head!'
'Oh, that's just her contact lenses.'
'But she's got bushy hair!'
'Oh, that's just her wig.'
'But she's got twenty ears!'
'Oh, that's just her mask.'
'But she's got one hundred earrings!'
'Oh, she's just likes jewellery.'
'But she's got four arms.'
'Six actually.
Now hurry up,
Auntie Ethel will eat us up if we're late.'

Kirsty Sutherland (7)
Olnafirth Primary School, Voe

Auntie Ethel, The Extraterrestrial

'But she's got a horn on the top of her head.'
'Oh, that's just her hairstyle.
Nothing to worry about.'

'But she only has one eye.'
'Oh, that's just her contact lenses.
Nothing to worry about.'

'But she's got one toe.'
'Oh, that's just the end of her foot.
Nothing to worry about.'

'But she has eight arms.'
'Oh, that's just her jumper.
Nothing to worry about.'

Lynsey Johnson (8)
Olnafirth Primary School, Voe

Auntie Ethel, The Extraterrestrial

'But she's got heated eyes.'
'Oh, that's just her glasses.
Nothing to worry about.'

'But she's got purple teeth.'
'Oh, that's just her lipstick.
Nothing to worry about.'

'But she's got slimy green skin.'
'Oh, that's just her make-up.
Nothing to worry about.'

'But she's got six antennae, sticking out of her head.'
'Oh, that's just her hairdo.
Nothing to worry about.'

Laynie Graham (6)
Olnafirth Primary School, Voe

Auntie Ethel, The Extraterrestrial

'But she has stripy hair.'
'Oh that's just her hairstyle.
Nothing to worry about.'

'But she has got four ears.'
'Oh, that's just her mask.
Nothing to worry about.'

'But she has one eye.'
'Oh, that's just her contact lenses.
Nothing to worry about.'

'But she has one toe.'
'Oh, that's just her shoe.
Nothing to worry about.'

'But she has flower hands.'
'Oh, that's just her holding flowers.
Nothing to worry about.'

Lauren Anderson (7)
Olnafirth Primary School, Voe

Auntie Ethel, The Extraterrestrial

'But she's got pink hair.'
'Oh, that's just her wig.
Nothing to worry about.'

'But she's got one hundred ears.'
'Oh, that's only her earrings.
Nothing to worry about.'

'But she's got one thousand mouths.'
'Oh, that's just her lipstick.
Nothing to worry about.'

Lois Sutherland
Olnafirth Primary School, Voe

Horses

One day I went for a walk
It was a lovely day,
I was walking past a paddock
Suddenly, horses galloped past
Mud splashing everywhere
Little foals running as fast as their legs would go.

Suddenly a little foal collapsed on the ground,
I ran over to it after, it tried to get up
It managed then it ran away
Following its mummy.

Running through the water
Splashing through the water
Splashing water at everyone
Drinking some then splashing all the other horses.

Beth Mitchell (11)
Ordiquhill Primary School, Banff

The Small Fish

The small fish that swims in the sea
Is only as big as a little green pea.
He swims through water at the speed of light.
When he meets a whale he's in for a fight.

The little fish eats up well,
Then he makes a bad smell.
He's afraid of the fat shark
And also afraid of dogs that bark.

The tiny fish stays well back,
Just in case he gets a big smack.
He likes to play with his Glen
And stays with his mum, she's called Pen.

Bradley Robertson (11)
Ordiquhill Primary School, Banff

Australia

Australia is a wonderful place,
Koalas climb up tall trees,
Kangaroos jump up and down
Along the open plain.

Birds of flight fills the air
Cockatoos fly up, up, up.
Many animals live there
Even duck-billed platypuses.

Kangaroos jump
Koalas climb,
Cockatoos fly,
Duck-billed platypuses swim.

Australia is a wonderful place,
Why not go and visit?

Lauren Middleton (11)
Ordiquhill Primary School, Banff

Little Fairy

Little fairy . . .
Fly so high in the sky.
Fly so gracefully,
Fly so happily.

Little fairy . . .
Spread out your golden wings,
Sprinkle your fairy dust,
Let down your silver hair.

Little fairy . . .
Shine like a star,
In the moonlit sky.

Little fairy,
Little fairy,
Be mine for evermore.

Rachel Hirsch (11)
Ordiquhill Primary School, Banff

Devil Sister

D evastating little things,
E ating, eating, chicken wings.
V ermin, rat's tail, eye of a toad.
I cy children on the road.
L ies she tells to her brother so sweet.

S tanding alone on the street.
I ncredibly nasty things I'll do
S o I think my dog needs a diddle do
T eams battle to be nastiest.
E veryone wants to be a baddie
R eally bad things I'll do to her.

Joseph Middleton (9)
Ordiquhill Primary School, Banff

Sports

S ports are fun to do
P ool is a slow sport
O ver the post, you have to kick the rugby ball
R ound the world, there are all kinds of sports
T ennis is a very fast sport
S wimmers are very fast.

John Verbiest (10)
Ordiquhill Primary School, Banff

Starry

S tarry is my pet cat, she's very fluffy and cute.
T hat she never runs away and that is that.
A lways likes to play with me and she is really friendly.
R eally likes sleeping,
R eally likes catching mice,
Y ou're the best cat ever.

Samantha Smith (9)
Ordiquhill Primary School, Banff

The Fizzy Drinker

A young man named Donald Fizzy,
Drinks as much as his pal Lizzy,
From beer to cola and lemonade
When he plays in his arcade.

Every day he drinks even more
He doesn't even fit his door,
He drinks and drinks and drinks and drinks
And soon he's too big, for ice rinks.

He drinks on Fridays, Saturdays, Sundays and even Mondays,
He even drinks on sunny days,
He drinks in the morning and drinks in the night
He never turns off his new light.

Fizzy is there and beer is here
He is stupid but he has nothing to fear,
He goes into a shop and buys even more
He does this while his head is sore.

Harry Edwards (11)
Ordiquhill Primary School, Banff

Teachers

Teachers here, teachers there
Teachers everywhere!
They go nag, nag, nag
And they brag, brag, brag!

The best one of all
She lives in the hall,
Her name is Mrs Hay
And she gives us fun all day.

So here's a reminder
Teachers can be kinder,
Open their kindness with a key
And just you wait and see!

Emma Duguid (10)
Ordiquhill Primary School, Banff

Sheep

Sheep
The furry little things
Only thing is they're so noisy.

They get so nervous when you're near.
So they shake with fear
You say, 'It's OK'
But they run away.

They're trapped in a barn
Inside the big farm
They will come to no harm.

Later on, they're put back in the field
So that the sheep can get peeled . . .
By sharp sheep shears.

Gabby Munro (11)
Ordiquhill Primary School, Banff

Mrs Hay

Mrs Hay, oh Mrs Hay
She gives us fun all day.
She lets us run and jump around
And hop and skip and climb and bound.

Mrs Hay, oh Mrs Hay
She loves the children all of the day.
She must be in a dilemma
When she has me and Emma.

Mrs Hay, oh Mrs Hay
She scoffs chocolate every day.
She also likes to go to the chippy
Where she finds her husband, the hippy.

Laura Smith (11)
Ordiquhill Primary School, Banff

Heather

Heather is the best.
She is better than all the rest.
She has dark brown eyes.
She never tells lies.
Together, we have so much fun.
Heather is always cheerful.
She is hardly ever tearful.
I have ten friends
But Heather is the bestest friend in the world and that is true.

Taylor Wollerton (9)
Ordiquhill Primary School, Banff

Friends

F is for fun
R is for races
I is for immoral, that my friends aren't
E is for everyone that are my friends
N is for never fight
D is for discuss, we always do
S is for something, we are always talking about.

Kenneth Cowie (9)
Ordiquhill Primary School, Banff

One Of My Pals

She's fluffy and sweet
Black and small
Small, small, small
Chirpy, happy, full of life
Always on the go,
She's in my pal and she is a chicken!

Jessica Philip (10)
Ordiquhill Primary School, Banff

A Map Of Feelings

I feel so sick of eating all of that chocolate
Wait, what am I saying, I want to go get some more.

I feel sad; my brother has left his empty room
Where the colours of his life will always stay
Along with feelings, I hope never to change or go away.

I feel lonely and bored, nobody's in
Even the dog's asleep, where do I begin?
The PS2's not satisfying, nothing is on TV
Maybe I should go and watch a long DVD.

I feel disappointed, I've been let down again
Why does this happen to me?
I just want to spend sometime with my friends and family
They always have excuses like I'm working, oh sorry.

All of these feelings bundled up inside me,
Like a colourful painting, sick, sad, lonely, disappointed
Ahh, they're only feelings.

Edward Ramsay (11)
Our Lady of the Annunciation School, Glasgow

Why?

Why when we wake up, we cannot see,
What the world really should be?
Why can't the world unite as one?
Why can't the world put down their guns?

Why can't we forget all of our troubles?
While the world's bad ideas double.
Why can't we live just one happy day?
That is all I'd like to say.

When will we wake up from our perfect little dream
And realise the world isn't as it seems?
Why, you might ask, do I question these things?
Because someone has to . . .

Rachel Sharp (11)
Our Lady of the Annunciation School, Glasgow

A Map Of Feelings

Lonely . . .
Dark and cold, the wind whipping all
The joy and happiness away.
The hard rain holding me down
Nothing to do, nothing to play.

Excitement . . .
It's the day, dogs and cats maybe
Even bats and butterflies in my stomach
Spots and dots, lots and lots.

Anger . . .
Shouting, screaming, round and round.
People knocking me to the ground.
Thumping, jumping, up and down.
Crying, dying, I'm being pushed
Down, down, down . . .

Rosa Halliday (11)
Our Lady of the Annunciation School, Glasgow

The Black Figure

I sit in my house reading a book.
I hear a noise, so I turn to look.
A big, black figure is crossing the hall,
He looks at me through his eyes, very small.

I hear a creak on the bathroom floor,
I go upstairs and open the door.
There is nothing there except the dark,
I look in the sink, there is a dirty mark!

I go to my bed, I am sound asleep
The pillows beside me are in a heap,
I am woken by a sudden shake
Oh . . .

Sean Coyle (9)
Our Lady of the Annunciation School, Glasgow

Summertime

S unset sparkling on the beach
U nbearable burning sand on my feet
M elted chocolate in my mouth
M any people shouting in the local park
E nergetic flavour of ice tea, freezing on my tongue
R ain dropping all over my car, on the motorway
T ime flying as I'm having fun on my summer holiday
I n all restaurants beautiful scent from lots of foods
M arshy, foamy, marshmallows tingling in my teeth
E dinburgh Castle's rock, underground growing upwards,
                                        towards the battlements.

Zain Aklhtar (11)
Our Lady of the Annunciation School, Glasgow

Flowers

F abulous colours on every petal
L ightly flowing in the breeze
O range, yellow, pink and blue
W et with morning dew
E verybody starting to look at the flowers
R unning down the path to pick them
S ilently putting them in a vase.

Molly McGovern (9)
Our Lady of the Annunciation School, Glasgow

Sydney

S ydney Harbour is filled with
Y achts sailing on the shimmering water
D own below the metal bridge
N ow ships pass through
E veryone gazes at the glimmering tiles of the Opera House roof
Y ou have to visit this marvellous place.

Owen Sweeney (10)
Our Lady of the Annunciation School, Glasgow

Christmas

C hristmas has everyone excited
H olly hanging from the Christmas tree
R ed ribbons shining amongst all the presents
I n the living room, the fire is on
S now is falling down, from the clear and cold sky
T he family is getting the dinner ready
M um is making the dessert
A s I sit down to eat, I hear
S leigh bells ringing!

Olivia Gough (9)
Our Lady of the Annunciation School, Glasgow

In Winter

I n winter, the snow is falling, lying thick on the ground
N ight is dark, you can't see a thing

W ind blows in your face, making you shiver
I nside by the fire, cosy and warm
N ow it's time for tea, I can't wait
T ea is ready, it smells great
E verybody had a wonderful day, in the snow
R unning around and having fun.

Aidan MacLeod (10)
Our Lady of the Annunciation School, Glasgow

Spring

S pring is the time when the daffodils appear
P etals start to open out
R ed blossoms pop out of the trees
I love the springtime
N ew buds grow on the trees
G reen grass rises under the soil.

Kamil Demroz (10)
Our Lady of the Annunciation School, Glasgow

Summertime Memories

S mall little animals, running and thriving
  While flowers in the meadows are blooming
U p above, the children are jumping and diving
  And others swim like sharks in the water
M any restaurants line the sand and sea,
  You can smell the most exotic food
M en enjoy a round of golf with their clubs and tee
  And women enjoy a manicure and pamper
E very night you go to a kids' club and play games,
  Create things and enjoy yourself
R emembering the souvenirs like a little tub of shells,
  Which I brought back for my best friend
T he food left me full, I could not eat anymore
  And the service was fantastic
I   went for a walk by the seashore;
  I could hear the seagulls squawking loudly
M y mind was relaxed by the lapping seawater
  Onto the light, golden sand
E xciting activities like looking at otters,
  Seals and dolphins at the aquatic centre.

Bernadette Campbell (11)
Our Lady of the Annunciation School, Glasgow

Think Of . . .

Think of no racism in the world.
Think of the people who have bad lungs from smoking and are
                                    about to die.
Think of the people who have suffered in hospital this Christmas time.
Think of the people who have not had a good Christmas.
Think of the poor people who have no food in the world.
Think of the people who do have food in the world.
Think of people being friends.
Think of the people who need peace in the world.
Think of the people who have lost their lives in the war.
Think of the people who are fighting other countries in the war.

John Middleton (9)
Our Lady of the Annunciation School, Glasgow

Poems Of Experience

Happiness
Children laughing, playing games
People passing, calling their names
Aunties and cousins coming home
In the house there's not a mouse.

Fear
In the dark with no one there
Hearing noises like a grizzly bear
Cutlery smashing, doors crashing
Washing machine vibrating as I am skating.

Excitement
She's finally come, this new little one
I can't wait to hold her, my new little sister
Why can't I see her? What's going on?

Stressed
So many things to do, I don't know where to start
Rushed off my feet
I feel like ripping out my heart
Need to go to work but first to tidy up
If only life was simple, then I'd know.

Love
When I get up in the morning, so many things to see
Open the window and hearing the birds high above the tree
I feel so new, not feeling blue
And now I know what to do.

Mairead McBride (11)
Our Lady of the Annunciation School, Glasgow

Walls

W e were all very happy to get on with our work
A t the time we were very excited
L ast summer in 2004 was when the walls were built
L osing the noise was great
S ome noise we could still hear.

Callum Higgins (10)
Our Lady of the Annunciation School, Glasgow

Poems Of Experience

Happy . . .
I feel like a puppy
Jumpy and excited!
Life is good
But sometimes it is not.

Sad . . .
I feel as low as the seabed
Boring and unnoticed!
Life is bad
But sometimes it is not.

Excited . . .
I feel so tempted
Dying to enter.
I think I'm going to burst
If I don't open the door!

Bored . . .
I feel like a cargo ship
Unexcited and lonely!
Once I reach my destination
I hope there's something to do!

Scared . . .
I feel like I'm on a merry-go-round
That's getting faster and faster!
I want it to stop
And I want to get off!

Luke Robertson (11)
Our Lady of the Annunciation School, Glasgow

Walls In The Hall

W ith quieter classrooms
A ll working hard
L ess noise more teaching
L earning and listening
S hh, I'm trying to work!

Jack Mullen (10)
Our Lady of the Annunciation School, Glasgow

Loudon Castle

I hear the *whoosh* of roller coasters
And the splash of water rides.
The whirring candyfloss machines
To make a sweet candy treat.

I feel happy and sad
When the ride is over,
I want to scream
When on the log flume.

I smell candyfloss
As it is made,
Exhaust fumes from all
Of the rides.

I see rides and more
On this fun day,
People waiting to
Have fun like me.

Andrew Brown (10)
Our Lady of the Annunciation School, Glasgow

Visualize

Visualize no water
Visualize no trees
Just think of our surroundings
Do they make you feel pleased?
Visualize a pool to swim in
No wars to fight in.
Visualize food to give out
No bullying to sort out.
Visualize a house to live in
Lots of rubbish in the bin.
Put all of that together
I wonder what you'll get
Peace with him and her.

Stuart McGibon (9)
Our Lady of the Annunciation School, Glasgow

Consider . . .

Consider peace in the world,
War that doesn't happen,
Weapons never made,
Consider a pool to swim in with friends all day,
No fighting or destroying.

Consider no smoking,
No one will die,
Friends forever.

Consider a life with no bad things,
It would be great.

Consider a friendly life,
A park with no litter,
Animals let free.

Consider this . . .
The world would be perfect for us!

Caitlyn Smith (9)
Our Lady of the Annunciation School, Glasgow

Poem Of Experience

Life has so many ups and downs,
So many feelings around,
We try to be happy and make other people happy too,
Sometimes it is hard to do.
So many problems to cope with
As you experience new things,
It would be great
If you had a magic wand.

Wouldn't life be great,
If we were happy all the time?
We can be happy or sad, bad or glad.
So many emotions, but only one you
So live life to the full and be cool.

Anne-Marie Roulston (11)
Our Lady of the Annunciation School, Glasgow

Suppose . . .

Suppose that we all shared
Peace around the world,
Happiness around us
No litter for a while.

Suppose there were no vandals
No smoking but there's good health.

Suppose we all had houses
So everybody got a place to live,
No bullying or teasing
Forgiveness we could give.

Suppose there were no vandals
No smoking but there's good health.

Suppose world wars were gone
No dying people now,
The world would soon get better
And we would all know how.

Suppose there were no vandals
No smoking, but there's good health.

Hannah Ruddy (9)
Our Lady of the Annunciation School, Glasgow

Fantastic Gymnastics

Bridge, full turn, handstand, cartwheel,
Oh, how really great I feel.

Leaping, prancing, gymnastics and dancing.

Run up quickly, then squat on,
Jump off, how has it gone?

Leaping, prancing, gymnastics and dancing.

I'm exhausted at the end of the day
'But it was worth it,' I quietly say.

Anna Kennedy (10)
Our Lady of the Annunciation School, Glasgow

Shawlands

S hoppers rushing to and fro, stop to
H ear the children's sweetest sound
A unts, uncles, mums and dads smile
W ith good cheer all around
L ights twinkling on the tree
A ngels glittering on the top
N ow's the time for peace and joy
D on't ever let it stop
S hoppers sitting, smiling, listening.

James Gallacher (11)
Our Lady of the Annunciation School, Glasgow

Memories Of Transport Museum Trip

M orning, people are excited
E verybody gets on the bus
M useum is full of school kids
O range cars on stands
R oaring sounds of children laughing
I got on a big train
E ating lunch with the class
S o that's our trip to the museum.

Andrew Howie (10)
Our Lady of the Annunciation School, Glasgow

Winter

W hite snow falling all around us
I n the park, people are sledging down the hill
N ew deep footprints in the garden, made by me
T he frosty cold nips my fingers and toes
E verything covered in blinding whiteness
R ivers are frozen with thick ice on top.

Mark Arlie (10)
Our Lady of the Annunciation School, Glasgow

Friendship

F or a friend, you're great fun
R iver hopping, having fun, getting wet or keeping dry
I n the river splashing or sploshing
E very day we meet and play
N othing would be better then dipping in again
D avid, my old friend from Spain, loved swimming
S ome friends come round to play
H ours of fun leaving us now because
I t's time to go and I say goodbye to
P als like Nicky and Sam.

Kathleen Buchanan (9)
Our Lady of the Annunciation School, Glasgow

Roller Coaster

R oller coasters are great, children laughing and rides whizzing
I n the carriage you hear wheels clicking and brakes screeching
D anger signs, *Do Not Put Hands Out Of Carriage* as flashing lights
start blinking
E veryone has a good day and on the bus home everybody
laughs happily.

Kieran McCallion (10)
Our Lady of the Annunciation School, Glasgow

Birthdays

B irthdays are fun
I like them a lot
R unning around
T oday is my birthday
H ooray! Remembering the
D ay that I was born
A nd what a day it is
Y ou would love to be here
S orry you didn't come.

Adam Cavanagh (10)
Our Lady of the Annunciation School, Glasgow

Science Centre

Our trip to the Science Centre,
Certainly was a day to remember.
Exploring the world of science and technology
In fun and exciting ways,
What a great way to fill our days.
I had fun in the IMAX cinema
As it took me on an adventure through the jungle
And showed me the fascinating world of bugs.
My classmates and I looked around the shop
Just for some interesting souvenirs of our trip
That really was the greatest bit.

Jason Docherty (10)
Our Lady of the Annunciation School, Glasgow

Think Of . . .

Think of no bullying, people would be happier.
Think of a world where there is no war, only peace.
Think of a world where litter is not found and cleanliness is all around.
Think of a world with no poverty,
Where people are treated nicely, no matter what they look like.
Think of this world, our world could be like it,
It could be real if everybody tried.

Balal Saleemi (9)
Our Lady of the Annunciation School, Glasgow

Memories

I remember my first Hallowe'en disco
Everyone dressed up.
Loud music playing,
Misty smoke in the air,
Crisps and drinks to savour.

Megan Darroch (10)
Our Lady of the Annunciation School, Glasgow

Think Of . . .

Think of all the people that died in the war.
Think of all the people that died for smoking.
Think of all the vandals, fighting and bullying.
Think of all the graffiti.
Think of all the poor people that have no food or water.
Think of all the friendships and love.
Think of the whole world sharing something.
Think of no war and peace in the world, wouldn't that be good?
Think if everyone had a house to live in and had food to eat,
Our world would have peace, love and friendship,
What a wonderful place to be!

Nadine Dolan (8)
Our Lady of the Annunciation School, Glasgow

Picture A World

Picture a world full of hatred.
Picture a world full of darkness.
Picture a world full of sharing.
Picture a world full of life.
Picture a world full of kindness and happiness all of the time.
Picture a world full of fighting.
Imagine what that would be like . . .

Lauren Crozier (9)
Our Lady of the Annunciation School, Glasgow

Think Of . . .

Think of all the people in the world that don't have a home.
Think of a world that has no wars, think of one that has peace.
Think of friendship, thinking of others and caring.
Think of no litter on our streets, how happy we would be.
Think of us all.
Think how happy we'd be if there was no bullying, just love.

Jennifer Marley (9)
Our Lady of the Annunciation School, Glasgow

Picture . . .

Picture there is no bullying
Just a world full of peace
No wars, nothing bad
Just kind people walking in the street.

Picture a clean world with no litter
No pollution and everyone has a house to live in
Nobody is homeless

Picture all the world with friends
The world full of friendship
Sharing, nobody is lonely or sad.

Namrah Akhtar (9)
Our Lady of the Annunciation School, Glasgow

A Map Of Feelings

Sadness, what a horrible feeling to have
I cry and puddles form.
While happiness falls off my body.
Why feel sad when you can feel happy?
You tell me because I don't know.
Lying in bed staring at a blank ceiling wondering what to fill it with.
Seeing other people laughing and having fun makes me feel empty.
The emotion happiness, no such emotion to me.

Kerry Connolly (11)
Our Lady of the Annunciation School, Glasgow

Football At Ibrox Training Ground

It was a sunny day last year in Primary 5
We saw Tommy Burns which was a surprise
When we started the fun had begun
We played football which was so much fun
When I scored I thought it was great
When the day ended I was upset.

Ryan Gallagher (10)
Our Lady of the Annunciation School, Glasgow

Suppose

Suppose everyone had a big pool to swim in,
Then they would be happy.
Suppose there was no litter at all,
Then all the things would be nice and clean.
Everyone sharing, suppose there was no fighting at all.
Everyone lived happily together.
Suppose there was no smoking and no cancer from smoking.
Suppose there was no bullying, just a wonderful world to live in.

Tayyabah Sardar (9)
Our Lady of the Annunciation School, Glasgow

Think Of . . .

Think of the world
No wars or bullying, we could change this world.
No litter or fighting.
Think of the world, hold hand after hand singing songs all day long.
Think of people not killing or dying
For the world to be safe and peaceful.
Think of a world which we can change
Where we could be for evermore happy.

Colette Armstrong (9)
Our Lady of the Annunciation School, Glasgow

Memories

I remember the badminton tournament
It was lots of fun until the sunset,
Children were stamping their feet to the beat
People cheering with laughter
Instructors shouting as they demonstrate
Teams clapping as they run round the pitch
It was a day I'll never forget.

Lucy Middleton (10)
Our Lady of the Annunciation School, Glasgow

Suppose . . .

Suppose there were no fights
And everyone reunites.
Suppose there was no litter
So that everywhere would glitter.
Suppose there were more police
To make the world safer.

Suppose there were no enemies
So that there was no trouble.
Suppose there were more friends
Everyone would be happy.
Suppose everyone was full of delight
There would not be anymore fights.

David Conkie (9)
Our Lady of the Annunciation School, Glasgow

Loudon Castle

Children waiting in the queue
People racing down the track
I see bumpers crashing into each other.
Children laughing out loudly
The sound of the roller coaster
Going *chua, chua, chua.*
The smell of the sticky candyfloss
The chips in the burger van
The cold metal bar from the roller coaster
The sticky walls of the bouncy castle
As nervous as a kitten
As excited as going on a plane
This is my favourite school day.

Grace Symes (10)
Our Lady of the Annunciation School, Glasgow

The Gymnastic Competition

A shiver of anticipation
Rolls down my spine,
As I head to school
On the last day of November.
The bus driver waits patiently
At the school gates for our team.
Everyone is determined to do their best
As the teacher hurries us onto the bus.
We all start to feel nervous
Because we are near the sports centre.
We all do well and have a chance to stretch and practise
Until it is time for our team to do their sequences.
We all do well and come back to crowds of friends
Asking how we got on.

Tony Mellon (10)
Our Lady of the Annunciation School, Glasgow

Dogs

Some dogs are playful
Other dogs race, some even hunt
Some people have dogs as pets.

You have to train a dog
So it will obey you
You can train it by the whistle
Or train it by your voice.

Having a dog is wonderful
You can name it and raise it
But you must take it for a walk
Every day!

Stefan Harte (9)
Our Lady of the Annunciation School, Glasgow